W9-ANO-680

MEGALIVING!
3O DAYS TO A PERFECT LIFE

By Robin S. Sharma, LL.B., LL.M.

A Special Edition

THE HAUNSLA CORPORATION
TORONTO • LONDON

MegaLiving! 30 Days to a Perfect Life
Copyright © 1994 by Robin Shilp Sharma. All rights reserved.

Canadian Cataloguing in Publication Data

Sharma,   Robin Shilp,   1964-
      Megaliving!   :   30 days to a perfect life

ISBN   0-9698225-0-2

1.   Success - Psychological aspects.   I.   Title

BF637. S8S53   1994   158' . 1   C94-931043-3

2nd Edition

Second Printing in Toronto, Canada

The author has made every effort to provide an authoritative study on this subject but is not providing any form of professional advice. It is recommended that the reader seek the assistance of a trained health professional where there are concerns as to a new program aimed at physical excellence.

Dedicated to my wonderful wife for her affection, to my brother for his inspiration and to my parents for showing me the way to MegaLiving! For Colby.

MEGALIVING!
30 DAYS TO A PERFECT LIFE

The Ultimate Action Plan for Total Mastery of Your
Mind, Body & Character

MegaLiving!   The 30 Day Program to a Perfect Life

<u>CONTENTS</u>   Page

Someone has well said, "Success is a journey, not a destination."
Happiness is to be found along the way, not at the end of the
road, for then the journey is over and it is too late. Today, this
hour, this minute is the day, the hour, the minute for each of us
to sense the fact that life is good, with all its trials and troubles
and perhaps more interesting because of them.

Robert R. Updegraff

Preface

This Revolutionary Book Will Change Your Life!

WE ALL have the potential for a Perfect Life. We all have the potential to achieve great things and live a life filled with joy, accomplishment and pure bliss. In some of us, this potential is slumbering deep inside, waiting only to be tapped and tested. The most noble of pursuits is to ignite this fire for personal mastery and life excellence. This book is the only tool you will ever need to do this.

There is a story of a weary traveller who met a wise sage on a mountain path high in the Himalayas. The traveller asked the old man where he could find the path which would lead him to the top of the mountain, his ultimate destination. The sage thought for a moment and then replied: "simply make certain that every single step is in the direction of the mountaintop and you will get there."

When your every thought and your every action is directed to your ultimate life goals, you become unstoppable and assured of great success and happiness. When you cultivate your mind, body and character, your life takes on powerful dimensions that you never thought possible. This book will provide you with all that you need to put far more living into your life.

Part I of MegaLiving! contains the leading principles of personal mastery and successful living. Part II will reveal to you the 200 MasterSecrets to making your life a magical dream while Part III contains the revolutionary 30 Day Program to a Perfect Life. This book will do wonders for you. Read it, apply it and share it. A Perfect Life is yours for the taking.

Robin S. Sharma, LL.M.
Toronto, Canada

THE ULTIMATE CHALLENGE

Some men see things as they are and say "why" ; I dream of things that never were and say "why not."

George Bernard Shaw

There are people who make things happen. There are people who watch things happen. And there are people who say "what happened?" The MegaLiving! program will make things happen in every aspect of your life and make it one that you will one day look back on with a true sense of accomplishment, fulfillment and lasting happiness. You have within you incredible powers to achieve everything you have ever dreamed about. With the effective tools that this book contains, you can change every single area of your life to make it truly great. MegaLiving!, which contains the revolutionary results of ten years of research into personal mastery, will put more living in your life and show you the secret path to a world filled with bliss, contentment and pure joy.

This book contains the master keys to successful living. You have the potential for a perfect life, this is certain. And if you commit yourself totally to this program for 30 days, you will receive the following benefits:

i)   mastery of your mind & lasting happiness
ii)   strategies for unshakeable confidence & Limitless Living!
iii) self-mastery in every area of your life
iv)   the powers of Kaizen & achieving your dreams
v)   an understanding of the Feelgood principle
vi)   boundless energy, enthusiasm & glowing health
vii) the secrets of longevity, health excellence & serenity

viii)   learn tools to reshape your life & become wealthy forever

ix)   possess proven techniques to take control of your destiny

Today is the first day of your perfect life, a life that is yours to shape into something truly wonderful and lasting. The past does not determine your future and a change towards personal excellence can happen in the blink of an eye if you will make a firm commitment to raising your life to its highest level. This program is for winners. The fact that you have purchased the program sets you apart from the vast majority of people and demonstrates that you wish to be a peak performer and condition your mind, body and character for excellence. Accept this challenge and dare to be great!

The First Step

Now shut your eyes, take five deep breaths and picture this scene taking place many years into the future: you are in an elegant dining hall, surrounded by those closest to you (who are dressed formally and beautifully). The candles on every table shimmer and the importance of the evening wafts through the air like the aromas from the kitchen. This is your testimonial dinner, an opportunity for the people who know you best to speak about you as a person, your achievements and your contributions. Reflect on what you would like them to say. At this dinner, in the twilight of your life, do you really want to hear that you have lived in an uninspired fashion, without passion and without concrete and lasting accomplishment. How would you feel on hearing that you did not even come close to meeting your mental, physical and spiritual potential? How would you feel on hearing that your dreams, however lofty, went unfulfilled and that you never did supercharge your life because you were always too busy trying to pay the bills and so very tired at the end of your day?

With MegaLiving! you are getting a second chance to powerfully change what you will hear at your testimonial dinner at the end of your life. This book is your most important wake-up call. If you follow the program daily, think about it seriously and apply the concepts, making a decision from the core of your heart to live your life in a magical and special way, you will hear very sweet sounds at your dinner. The guests will happily testify to your incredible personal power, dynamic personality, zest for life, goal achievement and life accomplishment. Becoming the very best you can be is life's most noble pursuit. This is what we are all here for and becoming the very best that you can be is the ultimate challenge of the MegaLiving! mastery program. Accept it with great energy and welcome yourself to the new reality of a Perfect Life.

THE POWER OF LIMITLESS LIVING

> *Deep within man dwell those slumbering powers; powers that would astonish him, that he never dreamed of possessing; forces that would revolutionize his life if aroused and put into action.*
>
> *Orison Swett Marden*

One of the most essential truths to recognize is the fact that the only limits on what we can achieve in life are those we create and place on ourselves. Circumstances are the creations of people and not the other way around. Think of the current limitations in your life, the obstacles preventing you from attaining your dreams and that state of bliss you so much desire. You have interpreted each one of these circumstances to be a roadblock or negative element in your life when this is not the case.

There is no such thing as a negative circumstance, only a circumstance that you may learn from and further develop yourself. If you set limits on yourself such as "I am too young to be a multi-millionaire", "I am not smart enough to be a world leader", "I am too lazy to start my own business" or " I don't have enough money to do this", your spirit will slowly die and you will fulfill your negative prophecy. Every event happens for a special purpose. Every problem is a special challenge from which we can learn and prosper to new heights of achievement. Every moment is perfect in nature, whether you realize it or not. If you recognize this age-old truth, you will accept every experience with gratitude and enthusiasm. If you don't, you will never realize the wonderful destiny that is yours for the taking.

The mind has immeasurable and vast potential that remains untapped in most people. It has been said that even the best conditioned thinkers use only about 25% of their minds. What happened to the remaining 75%? Indian yogis have disciplined their minds to the point that they can control so-called involuntary processes such as heartbeat, digestion and nervous functioning. Mothers whose children have fallen under cars have, in the heat of the moment, lifted the vehicle to save their little ones. Seventy year old men have run marathons and climbed mountains. There are simply no limits for a person who accepts no limits.

The human mind and spirit can perform miracles if properly used and conditioned for excellence. And yet most human minds remain uncultivated, unexplored and unchallenged. Limited thinking patterns must be exploded and you must exert your tremendous mind strength to develop the habit of Limitless Thinking. Throw off the shackles of your old thinking patterns. The first step to a life full of wonders is to see that your outside world begins with your inside world and every single thought must be one that will take you farther along the path of a perfect life. Your thoughts can create magic and every thing you have ever wanted. Today's thoughts build tomorrow's dreams.

Mahatma Ghandi, a frail, weak man roused hundreds of millions of his countrymen and brought down an empire with passive resistance. His disciplined thinking had no limits and he would not allow disempowering thoughts to spoil his dream. Arnold Schwarzenegger was a young man when he entered the gym for the first time. He had skinny legs, a shrunken chest and small shoulders. Shortly after his first bodybuilding session he turned to another bodybuilder and said he would be Mr. Universe in five years. This is a man who refuses to accept limitations on what he can do and the success that he will meet with as he bounds through the rose garden of life. As Napoleon Hill wrote in the wonderful book, *Think and Grow Rich* : "whatever the mind of man can conceive and believe he can achieve."

So an immediate challenge to you is to weave your new habit of Limitless Thinking today. MegaThinking!, the powerful habit of thinking without any limitations on what you can do, have, feel and enjoy, arrives through gradual and steady conditioning of the mind. Positive thinking is pure habit and is not easy at first if you have allowed weeds to take over the garden of your mind. But the prosperity mindset can be developed as any other habit. Habit is like a cable; each day the action is taken, the cable becomes stronger until the point is reached where it is unbreakable. This is the point that you must and will reach with this program.

Now sit down and identify on a piece of paper those thoughts and thinking patterns that have held you back and limited your life in the past. Awareness of your limitations is the first stage in banishing them from your mind. What beliefs have kept you from success, happiness, love and self-mastery? Note them and make a decision to eradicate them from your mind. It will be hard at first and you will wish to give up but they *will* soon dry up if you will them away. Once you note the limiting thoughts and consciously remove them from your consciousness, it is key that you replace them with an alternative that energizes you, motivates you and fills your dreams with hope and passion. Picture yourself in your mind's eye as you hope to be, having all you've ever dreamed of having. Make a "Dream List" of everything you desire in your lifetime. It might seem silly and wasteful to think such positive and powerful thoughts in your current circumstances but there is phenomenal power in believing and in positive mental pictures.

THE PROMISE OF MegaLiving!

> *Infinite riches are all around you if you will open your mental eyes and behold the treasure house of infinity within you. There is a gold mine within you from which you can extract everything you need to live life gloriously, joyously and abundantly.*
>
> Joseph Murphy, Ph.D. , *The Power of Your Subconscious Mind*

The MegaLiving! 30 day program for self-mastery is not a fad or quick-fix course that will sustain your interest for a couple of weeks and then take its place in the closet with all the other personal development manuals you have bought in the past. It is a detailed piece of research containing the secret gems for life mastery prepared by studying success for over a ten year period. You have dynamite in your hands whether you realize it or not.

MegaLiving! is a complete program for the transformation of your mind, body and character starting today. You have a golden opportunity to be a true master of yourself and your existence. You can make your world the bed of roses that you have always dreamed of, the decision is yours alone. If you want this kind of a magical existence, the golden key is to remember that your mind is the sole author of your destiny and your success.

Past experiences, failures or trouble spots have nothing to do with the potential that exists within you. If anything, past failure has made you far wiser and stronger than you would have been without the benefit of the experience. Today, and every day, take complete charge and responsibility for your life and all that is in it. If you don't have enough money and want more, decide to make changes and take massive action to realize your dreams. If you want better health, it can be yours. But it will not just come to you by chance. You must develop a plan of attack and then take small daily steps in the direction of your goal.

Let me ask you a few questions and please take the time to answer them (doers are the only achievers):

Question	Answer

Do you want to be a champion in life?
Do you want more mental power?
Do you want perfect health?
Do you want more energy & vitality?
Do you want to add fun to your life?
Do you want to fulfil your dreams?
Do you want more serenity in life?
Do you want more adventure in life?
Do you want a powerful character?
Do you want to live longer?
Do you seek self-mastery & passion

If you answered "YES!" to any one of these questions, this program will be invaluable to you and your quest for a perfect life. MegaLiving! blends the latest physical mastery and healthy lifestyle techniques with ancient strategies for mental conditioning and character building to offer a fully balanced owner's manual for your mind, body and spirit. It is a holistic approach to personal growth that, if applied daily and with sincere conviction, will ensure that you will soar to heights higher that you ever dreamed possible. Ignite your desire and stoke the fire in your belly for you will soon be MegaLiving!

Once you truly commit yourself to the program, you will appreciate how easy and fun it is. Most importantly, the 30 Day program will bring very dramatic results in each of the areas that matter most in your life. You will view the world differently. You will understand the magnificence of it and the tremendous opportunities that live in every moment. You will break free of the thick haze that most people live in and rise above the average to the path of perfection.

EXCELLING WITH THE PROGRAM

For the purposes of action nothing is more useful than narrowness of thought combined with energy of will.

-Henri Frederic Amiel

There are no shortcuts to the success and pleasure you will receive when MegaLiving! becomes your habit. "Patience, the essential quality of a man" wrote Kwai-Koo-Tsu. To get the exceptional results the program can deliver, the following points are important:

<u>Follow the program daily</u>: Reserve judgement on the success of the MegaLiving! program for 30 days. Do not become discouraged and lose your enthusiasm. Studies have shown that it takes at least 21 days for perceptible changes to appear in your life when you are trying to make improvements. Each day you follow the program, you will feel better, perform better & achieve more. By making small, daily changes on a gradual and consistent basis, your enthusiasm will increase as will the visible results.

A missed day does not mean you remain where you are. Missing a day will mean that you are falling backwards. Again, do not miss even one day of this revolutionary program- daily study and application of its principles is key to dramatic success and conditioning your mind, body & character. Some days will be harder than others. Discipline is built by following through on these "low energy" days. Soon they will be few and far between. This is the nature of will.

<u>Work hard on the program</u> : This is your best chance to reshape your world and become an elite performer on the playing field of life. Use the Success Log provided at the end to chart your daily progress, your thoughts, your aspirations and successes. Throughout the day, revise the principles and use the strategies provided. On the subway, in the car and in the shower, mentally repeat your commitment to mastery of all areas of your life.

<u>Publicize your commitment to MegaLiving!</u>: Tell your family and friends that you will follow through with the program and that they will notice dramatic changes in you in the future. Inform them of your goals. This is an excellent way to get leverage and motivation on the dreams and desires you hold. No one wants to look like a failure or like a person with no willpower & persistence and a little pressure will stimulate you to massive positive action.

By implementing the 30 Day MegaLiving! program daily and making small, consistent changes, your personal energy and desire will snowball and soon take on enormous dimensions. By charting the progress in your SuccessLog, your interest and enthusiasm will increase. And by publicizing your commitment to the course, you will get tremendous leverage for your ultimate aspiration: a perfect life and total self-mastery.

> *Man is made or unmade by himself. In the armoury of thought he forges the weapons by which he destroys himself. He also fashions the tools with which he builds for himself heavenly mansions of joy, strength and peace. By the right choice, and true application of thought, man ascends to divine perfection. By the abuse and wrong application of thought, he descends below the level of the beast.*
>
> James Allen, *As a Man Thinketh*

YOUR COMMITMENT TO SELF-MASTERY: THE POWER OF KAIZEN

Kaizen means improvement and there is no more noble nor important pursuit than self-improvement. As Confucius said many years ago: "good people strengthen themselves ceaselessly." Consistent and constant improvement in all areas is essential. You must apply the kaizen principle on a daily basis to condition your mind to peak performance. It has been said that the mind is a terrible master but a wonderful servant. By seeking to improve your mind and condition it to excellence of thought, this wonderful servant will most certainly bring you all the peace, prosperity and joy that you are now searching for.

Study any great success story and you will undoubtedly learn of their commitment to kaizen. They will be dedicated to small, daily improvements in the key areas of their lives and becoming the very best that they could be.

Walt Stack, an 80 year old man who runs the entire length of the Golden Gate Bridge in California every day, come rain or shine was asked how did he keep his teeth from chattering on those cold mornings. "I leave them in my locker" he replied wryly. To be great you must act great. Nothing can stop a person who refuses to be stopped.

Most people spend their whole lives struggling for a little happiness against a current of problems or difficulties, hoping to see a small glimpse of blue sky against the mass of dark clouds which seem to encircle their lives. These people never realize the magic secret of true happiness: one must rise above the clouds to see the blue sky rather than constantly trying to push the clouds aside. They will always be there but anyone who conditions their mind and body to the correct degree will rise above any clouds to live with lasting bliss in the blue sky of life. Dedicate yourself to such self-enhancement, each and every day of your life. Become a champion. Remember, happiness is a method of travelling through this wonderful world and not a destination, a place you arrive at in the future. A time will definitely come when your personal power takes you to a place where you have real freedom and joy. This is a place where all dreams come true. This is the place of self-mastery. This is a place called MegaLiving!

Excellence in Personal Mastery

Does you mind sometimes feel like a bowl of pudding? Are you easily distracted or pulled away from important tasks that require powerful thought and concentration? Do you lack will-power and discipline and get into the same limiting, destructive thought patterns over and over? If so, you must exert your personal influence (which may currently be dormant inside of you) to exercise and condition your mind. The mind is similar to the muscles of the body: if you do not use it and give it a good workout every day, it will become flabby. A flabby mind allows weak thoughts to enter. Weak thoughts drain your energy and limit your actions. Limited, unproductive actions prevent you from being the best and attaining all of your desires.

Sir Issac Newton, the father of classical physics had an exceptional ability to concentrate on a particular problem from morning until it was solved late in the evening. This mental giant said that "if I have done the public any service, it is due to patient thought." What most people do not realize is that anyone can enhance the level of their mental functioning. You can become more mentally agile, improve your memory well beyond its current level and become a smarter mental athlete. But you must go into training as does any serious athlete. You must place your mind on a regime designed to fire up the brain and dramatically reshape it. The MegaLiving! program will do this for you if you follow it strictly and passionately. While the mental aerobics listed in the 30 day Megaliving! program and the brain-building exercises appearing in the course take you to new intellectual heights, the important idea to hammer home at this point is that you must set aside one hour each day, at the very least, to renew and revitalize your mind, body and spirit. There are 168 hours in a week, can you not find 60 minutes in a day to take care of the very tool that will take you to the success that you desire so much? You may say that you are very busy and cannot afford to take this time off. In reality, you cannot afford to miss this essential period to sharpen your mind, condition your body and feed your spirit.

What should you do in this one hour "rekindling" session that is so very important? The answer is clear: practice self-mastery, kaizen. Although the program lists particulars, what is key is that you spend some time on each of the following, each day (get up an hour earlier or do it in the evening, it will be one of the most magical decisions you have ever made):

1. Personal Development

Personal development is really any activity that gives you knowledge on improving your life and all its elements. It may be reading an inspirational book like *The Power of Positive Thinking* or *Think and Grow Rich*. It may involve the exceptionally valuable habit of listening to motivational tapes while you drive to work or sit on the subway. It could be digesting a hot book on diet and health such as *Fit For Life* or reading the latest text on managing your time.

The key is that you start to tap the incredible amount of information that is out there on improving your life. It is amazing to learn of the strategies and techniques available which would do wonders for most peoples lives if they only knew about them. All we need is a single powerful idea to change our lives for the better. What distinguishes successes from failures is that the successes constantly thirst for new ideas and knowledge. Successful people are hungry for anything that will give them an edge in life's wonderful game. The answers to a life of perfection and bliss are out there and as abundant as the air we breathe. Be open to them and be on the lookout for them at all times.

Readers are leaders and you will be a true leader once you get into the habit of being devoted to personal development on a daily basis. Miss a meal but don't miss your daily personal improvement time.

2. Physical Fitness

You must spend at least 30 minutes daily cultivating the perfect health which lies deep inside of you. Daily exercise, as you have heard so many times, is the easiest and one of the most effective ways to arrive at the state of personal excellence. If someone said he would give you the secret of longevity, super energy and serenity, you would do almost anything to get it. Well, the secret is yours now: exercise every day and you will see a vitality enter your life that will surely change it very dramatically and ignite your spirit.

A little exercise every day will make you more relaxed, improve your concentration and dramatically improve your inner world. With the abundance of energy a fitness program surely provides, you will be able to take those positive steps in the direction of your dreams. Swim, run, walk through the woods, take up karate, learn how to waterski, play squash, bicycle, do some gardening, get some fresh air, rollerblade, have fun at aerobics but get out of that life-sapping habit of sitting on a couch and watching TV all night!

How will you feel when your friends say you look marvellous and years younger. How will you feel when you have the stamina to work all day, then come home and laugh and play with your family and later, after a brisk walk around your neighborhood, you slip off to your den to spend a couple of hours on an activity that will really make your life great. Trust me, physical excellence precedes mental excellence.

3. Relaxation

The body and mind are like a high performance racing car. It will perform at its peak if it remains cool and well-oiled. Relaxation is essential for the body and without it, the body slowly deteriorates and loses its vitality. "The soul that moves in the world of the senses and yet keeps the senses in harmony... finds rest in quietness" notes the ancient Indian text *The Bhagavad Gita*. The body and mind are intimately linked and if your body is tense, your mind will be tense, unfocused and agitated. Stress hampers your creativity and intellect in very serious ways.

The key is to simply spend some time every single day on relaxation and quieting your mind. It will be the best decision you have ever made and will lead to more effectiveness in all the important areas of your life. Every peak performer, from Michael Jordan to the President of the United States recognizes the value of a calm, disciplined and relaxed mind. So must you and it can be achieved by a daily period of relaxation. Ancient deep breathing techniques, the tremendous value of stretching and yoga, meditation, contact with nature, self-massage and mental tranquility exercises are all part of the MegaLiving! 30 day program which you will immerse yourself in later. For now, appreciate the 17th century philosopher Robert Burton's sage advice:" a quiet mind cureth all." Relax your mind and body daily, jump start your life & soar to your highest potential.

THE NATURE OF THE MIND: THE ULTIMATE SUPERPOWER

> *Thought is a vital, living force, the most vital, subtle and irresistible force that exists in the universe. ... Thoughts are living things.*
>
> *Swami Sivananda*

To unleash the tremendous power reserves which currently sleep within you, it is critical that you first become aware of the nature of the mind. You are given an owner's manual for everything but that which is most important to you-your mind. In school, we are taught how to do complex Algebra and the capitals of far away lands that we may never visit. What about the nature of our greatest gift, our mind? The first step to personal mastery and successful living is to learn how to run your mind like a winner. The second step is to understand once and for all that your mind can create magic in your life if you only would let it. The only limitations in your life are those that you consciously set. When you think without limits and dream great dreams, wonderful things happen and powerful forces are set into play.

To run your mind like a peak performer, study the following 10 Golden Rules for Mental Mastery:

1. The level of your success is determined by what you think every second of every day. Today's thoughts will serve to build your dreams of tomorrow.

2. Your outer world reflects your inner world. If you want to change your life, you must start by changing the thoughts you put into your mind.

3. You alone are responsible for what you think. Most importantly, you can change the way you think and remove any negative thinking habits by the daily practice of mental discipline. Thinking patterns are habits and, like all habits, they can be changed when you strongly desire to change them and take concrete action towards your goal.

4. A supersuccessful mindset does not happen in a day. You have to work hard on it. But in 30 days of daily, concentrated practice, you will note astonishing changes in the way you think, feel and act.

5. One of the great keys to a better life is to change your self-image. Our self-image is determined by the mental pictures we constantly run through our mind. When you change the pictures to show what you really want to be and have in your world, your self-image also changes dramatically. This in turn leads to greater confidence and belief in your abilities. Goals are then easily achieved.

6. Anything you faithfully and honestly believe you can achieve, you will achieve if you take persistent action in that direction. Constantly keep your dreams at the front of your mind. Repeat them all day, every day. Never, ever let go of them. People with far less than you have have achieved great feats.

7. The Law of Attraction is the dominant law of the mind. What you think about and believe is what you attract into your life. People who are happy and motivated attract such people into their world. People with a positive expectation of super success will attract opportunities to allow them to arrive at this destination.

8. Your subconscious mind plays a particularly great role in the outcome of your life. You must learn how to use it for maximum achievement. Again, mental pictures and verbalization play a big role in stimulating your subconscious mind.

9. Your mind has the capacity to hold only one thought in its focus at any one time. Using this knowledge, you must ensure that each thought is a valuable and positive one. If a negative, disempowering thought does enter, quickly replace it with a good one. As you develop the habit of thinking useful, energizing thoughts, weak ones will no longer hold any power.

10. There is a Success Mechanism inside of your mind which craves positive stimulation. It awaits your instructions. When you realize this and start setting big, great goals for yourself, it will spring to life and seize all

opportunities to allow you to get to where you want to go.

Scientific researchers are discovering the virtually limitless capacity of the brain and that we generally use only about 20% of its potential on any given day. Human beings are designed to have perfect health and a perfect mind but, during the course of our lives, we learn to sabotage ourselves and exclude perfection.

As a baby, you were in the ideal performance state to achieve excellence. Did you fear public speaking, starting a successful business or skydiving? Of course not. As a child, you dreamed of becoming a movie star, an astronaut or a president. What happened? You have been exposed to people and beliefs after birth that have taught you that some things were beyond your ability. You were told that regular people did not move into the White House and you best focus on making a living and paying the bills because this was what life was really about. So gradually, the spark of a limitless reality died. Gradually, your worldview shrunk from imagining the thrills of greatness to paying the bills and cutting the grass. But you can return to the winning mindset and rekindle the fire that lies deep inside of you. To do this, the mind must be conditioned through the regular exercises which form part of the MegaLiving! program.

It has been said that you can change your life with a single idea- if it is the right one. This requires desire, persistence and practice and it will not come in a week or ten days. It certainly *will* come though as long as you take action now! You can transform your life and have everything you have ever wanted when it does. As the age old expression says "sow a thought, reap an action, sow an action, reap a habit, sow a habit, reap a character, sow a character, reap a destiny!"

It is also essential to appreciate the incredible power of focus. Have you ever noticed that when you buy a new car it suddenly seems that everyone in the world has the same one? Whenever you hear a new name, it is suddenly everywhere. This is the magical power of focus. The first step to excellence is awareness and your focus is the laserbeam of awareness. What you focus on shapes your life.

Once you make a clear decision to focus on something, opportunities seem to appear from out of the blue. For example, if you focus carefully on seeking knowledge for personal development, you will start to see information on this subject is everywhere, you simply did not notice it because you were focused on other things. Another example is in your own home. Walk into your favorite room and look at every object in the room. You will notice things that you may not have noticed in the past because you never really took the time to concentrate on them.

Many people dislike their jobs or their relationships. This is simply because they focus on the negative aspects of each. They don't like their boss and are not thrilled by the work and continually focus on these points until a negative association is formed. But things change when you simply ask them if their offices are comfortable, are there others who don't even have jobs and are on the street, if they have a good pension plan, whether they enjoy the good friends they have made through work or whether the money is pretty good. Every experience has many positive elements. If you focus on these, you will excel and reach higher planes. This is one of the most important success secrets. If you dwell on the negative aspects of life, you will get nowhere fast. Get into the habit of positive focusing today. You will reap huge rewards.

Once you make the decision to focus on a perfect life and master of all its components, you will find signs of excellence and positivity everywhere. This is where knowledge comes in. Once you are on the road to self-mastery and are focusing on all that is good in your world and that which is required to make it even better, knowledge will catapult you to the highest level. When an unquenchable thirst for knowledge is cultivated, you start to see the abundant strategies, techniques and ideas that will get you to where you want to go.

Remember this ancient truth: you can accomplish *anything* in your life with the right knowledge. Knowledge provides the means for achieving all objectives and the training to meet all goals. Knowledge provides answers which if focused on consistently and applied correctly lead to mastery in every life facet. If you want to become a multi-millionaire in three years, no matter how much you pray and think positively, it will not happen if you do not take any action. But if you set a goal (i.e., $3 million in 3 years), develop a plan (create a hot product) and then seek out all available knowledge on the product itself, the market, others who have succeeded in business, the mindset of winners and other such topics, you will quickly know what strategies others have followed to make millions. This will then give you the thoughts and beliefs on which you must focus to meet with success.

If you want to achieve any goal, the path is simple: seek out all available knowledge and then apply it massively. Find someone else who has achieved that goal, ask her how she did it, what books did she read, what thoughts did she think, which people did she talk to, what did she do when she woke up in the morning and throughout the day. This technique is known as Success Imaging. You must become a mirror image of the person who has succeeded in the activity you desire excellence in- be it running a country or a local bakery. You must emulate their physiology (walk like them, talk like them, eat like them) and their psychology (think like them and react like them).

By taking these steps, you are bound to get the same results that they have received. Become an explorer in the galaxy of knowledge that is available to anyone with a library card. You can learn any language, skill or concept through knowledge and proper coaching. Get in the daily habit of talking to new people and tapping their minds. Ask question after question. Read new books and listen to tapes on the subjects which are the center of your focus. You will soon gain unshakable confidence and unstoppable momentum.

Just as a butterfly must shed her cocoon before she flies out into the deep blue sky, you too must make an energetic effort to shed the cocoon of limitations that has enveloped your life and prevented you from self-mastery and life excellence. And no matter how successful you presently are, how happy you are and how much wealth you currently possess, there is more out there for you. Bill Gates of Microsoft fame became a billionaire in his early thirties, J.F.K. the President of the United States in his forties. You have all of the qualities of such people, they may just not be developed to their true potential. Shatter the beliefs which cause you to think that you are not well educated enough, intelligent enough, fit enough, rich enough or happy enough to make this life your masterpiece. This minute, make the ultimate decision of your life and become aware of all those thoughts and beliefs that you have allowed to hamper your performance. Get ready for the mind-body training that is the essence of this program. Get ready for MegaLiving!

DISCIPLINE & WILL-POWER: THE GOLDEN KEYS TO THE GATES OF SELF-MASTERY

> *Man is still responsible. He must turn the alloy of modern experience into the steel of mastery and character. His success lies not with the stars but with himself. He must carry on the fight of self-correction and discipline. He must fight mediocrity as sin and live against the imperative of life's highest ideal.*

> Frank Curtis Williams

The most important initial ingredients of self-mastery and life excellence are discipline and will-power. With them, you will have taken the first step to a perfect life. They are the qualities that ensure your success. With discipline and mental persistence, you *will* find the means to your ends. You *will* have the personal toughness to apply the principle of kaizen and to develop yourself to reach your goals. Discipline allows you to follow the MegaLiving! program daily to unleash the sleeping potential inside of you. It provides you with the character strength to set aside watching the television and other time wasting activities in favor of those that will truly make a lasting difference in your life.

The Magic of Discipline for Life-Mastery

There are 168 hours in a week. Discipline and mental toughness ensure that this time is well spent and your life retains the balance of physical fitness, mental conditioning, character building, professional pursuits, social activities and pure adventure that will foster its greatness. Most importantly, the development of discipline ensures that you are always focused on your life goals and moving powerfully and consistently towards them.

Erasmus said "a nail is driven out by another nail; habit is overcome by habit." The heart of discipline is indeed habit. Discipline and will-power, like the biceps, are muscles to be conditioned and built-up. Success in any endeavour requires a focused mind and regular application. Without the power that discipline brings, no dream can be realized. Without will-power, you become a victim to the evils of procrastination, laziness and sloth.

Discipline and will-power deliver you to the highest level of living possible and though it might seem difficult to develop at the outset, once these muscles are consistently exercised into a habit, stunning results appear and hard tasks become easy. With discipline you can raise your standards of physical fitness, tap into the amazing reserves of knowledge, start and finish major tasks, control your diet, triple your energy level, build your character to have a more fulfilling life and enhance your personal relations. Discipline will shape the tremendously important habit of mind control and positive thinking and free you from worry. Discipline will dramatically improve your confidence levels and your productivity as you start to put first things first.

Without discipline, or at least a clear desire to build it, you are lost and are destined to be the servant to your mind rather than having your mind serve you. Rather than having mental toughness and agility, disempowering thoughts will creep into your brain freely, zapping you of your personal power and redirecting your attention from your goals to useless activities that might feel fun but will offer no value in the long run.

One of the best personal growth objectives anyone can set is to develop their discipline/will-power muscles. In his excellent book, *Will-Power*, Raymond De Saint-Laurent writes that "the man of character is one who selects a reasonable objective and never gives up pursuing it so long as he has not reached his goal." Once you are aware how to use your will, no dream will elude you. Your mind will not be swayed like a leaf in the Fall wind. Once you have a worthy desire, you will exert a totally concentrated mind and effort on it. People will not move you from the path of success nor be able to discourage your aspirations. Here are some of the essential points to note about will-power:

i) **Winners Are Disciplined!** Every person who has met with great success in life and created their perfect life has had an abundance of discipline and will-power. Your world will change with these magical qualities but you must first understand that they are currently dormant within you. These priceless gems simply need to be polished and refined before they bring you riches that you have never imagined.

ii) **Use Your Will!** The secret to conditioning your discipline/will-power muscles is incredibly simple: use them or lose them! Nature is consistent in its principles. To increase your biceps, exert them and push them to the limit regularly. Soon they will grow strong. Exert and push your memory to remember more, it will soon grow strong. Exert and push your imagination. Visualize the perfect you and feel that you are that person. You will soon grow strong and become that image. This is the way of your discipline/will-power muscles also. The key is to push them and exert them. They will definitely blossom beyond your expectations.

iii) **Have Big Hopes and Think Good Thoughts!** Even if you now think you are weak, lethargic and apathetic, remember the essential truth that there is a sparkling spring of will-power bubbling within you. With the proper cultivation, that the MegaLiving! 30 day program provides, the spring will explode into an unstoppable current!

iv) **Become a Will-Power Warrior!** The MegaLiving! program will teach you how to wage a war against impulses that drain your energy and keep your limitless potential at bay. You must examine yourself carefully and become aware of the disempowering thoughts that you have conditioned into your way of thinking. Then you must stop thinking them and repeat to yourself, over and over, that it is these thoughts that are keeping you from perfect health, perfect wealth and a truly magical existence.

One of the most common "diseases" in our modern world is fatigue. People rush to work, are busy all day and run home to have a quick meal and drop into their favorite couch and doze off in front of their television. The most common excuse for not doing something important has now become "but Honey, I was too tired." People who once had lofty ambitions about becoming famous and changing the world for the better now crave nothing more than a night with 8 hours of good sleep. Our society is paralyzed by its tired citizens who lack the energy to achieve what they need to achieve in order to make their lives memorable. Would you be shocked to learn that, generally, the "fatigue disease" is nothing more than an illusion? To illustrate this essential truth, think about the last time you were at the office or at home reading something boring and dull. Think of how you really disliked having to plod through the material and think of how tired you felt reading it. Your head started to bob and you actually nodded off a few times. If only you could have a little nap you thought. Then, you were interrupted by a ringing phone or a friendly colleague who dropped by. All of a sudden, the drowsiness and fatigue vanished. You felt alert and vibrant again. You were really not tired at all but, rather, had created this state because you were not interested in the subject and, more importantly, had not developed the habit of disciplining yourself to push on through the material.

Once you start to discipline you mind, it will work wonders for you. Mental and physical fatigue will be a thing of the past. Worry and negative thinking is the greatest cause of fatigue known. A wandering mind will do more to make you tired than a 10 mile run. The mind is like a thousand volt battery. It starts the day fully charged and full of energy. Then, as the day goes by, 100 hundred volts are lost worrying about the bills. Another 200 volts are lost thinking about some past event that is really not important and that you know you should not even think about. Another 300 volts are lost by daydreaming about a vacation that you want to take but cannot afford. Soon all your energy is gone and you feel like you need a rest.

The first step to eliminating mental fatigue is to discipline every thought in your mind. Make very certain that each one is an optimistic, positive one. Then, with the habit of discipline, start to realize that you have an incredible energy reserve that is simply waiting to be tapped. Realize that the fatigue is your own creation. Break the habit of fatigue. When the tired feeling starts to take hold, keep focused on the task at hand. Just as a runner gets a second wind on a long run, your mind will get a second wind if you exert your discipline muscles and stick with the job you are doing. It will not be easy at first. But you must be strong and not seek to escape the task you may be finding dull and unpleasant. Soon your discipline will take over. Things you had trouble doing will become easy. Large goals seem attainable and your confidence increases. You become mentally stronger and happier.

It has been said that successes do those things that failures don't like to do even though they also find them unpleasant. One of the world's greatest success tips is that all of life's happiness comes from achieving goals. When you look back on your life, what will make you happy will be the great things you have done, the superb family you raised, the prosperous business you created, the places you travelled to and the exciting books you have read. You will not look back and find a sense of accomplishment in the television shows you watched or in the weekend mornings that you slept until noon. Your life will be elevated by one thing and one thing alone: achievement. This does not mean that you must strive to make 10 million dollars or build a house in Bermuda. Achievement and life success can appear in peace of mind and a well-developed spiritual life. The key is simply to achieve. Discipline and will-power will make you a success. Cultivate them and treat them as your golden gifts.

THE FEELGOOD PRINCIPLE & BELIEF SYSTEMS: UNLEASHING VITALITY

Be not afraid of life. Believe that it is worth living,
and your belief will help create that fact.

William James

The MegaLiving! program is far more than simple positive thinking. It is a holistic program designed to raise your life to its highest level at every facet. Over 30 days, you will learn the secrets to unleashing the exceptional powers of your mind and supermemory, strategies for maintaining the perfect health state and longevity and techniques to build a stronger, more productive character full of integrity and an abundance/prosperity mentality.

If you take anything away from this revolutionary course, remember this one enduring truth known as the Feelgood Principle: everything you have ever done in your life, every action you have ever taken has been taken as a direct result of your powerful need to feel good. What you focus on throughout the day, what you eat and drink, the people you associate with and the books you read all arise out of your desire to feel good. The evil of procrastination comes about through the application of the Feelgood Principle: you derive more pleasure by sitting on the couch doing nothing than becoming physically fit or finishing that report for work that could really give your career the boost that it deserves.

When you eat too much, sleep too much, smoke too much, you are applying the Feelgood Principle. You are taking these negative steps because they make you feel good. Think of all the things in your life that you know you should not do. Why do you continue to do them? Awareness is the first step to excellence and once you become aware of the magic of the Feelgood concept you will then have a particularly strong tool with which to transform your behaviour and world.

List on a piece of paper all the activities that are preventing excellence in your life. Do you fight with others, worry too much, see the obstacles in life rather than the endless possibilities? Are you scared to exercise? All limiting activities can be changed in a relatively short period of time with the correct strategies. Perhaps the most powerful tool is simply to start applying the Feelgood Principle for positive rather than negative ends.

Here is the technique to make powerful, lasting transformations in your life:

Step 1: The Decision

Today make the decision that you *need* to change your behaviour. It has caused you too much pain in the past and it must stop now! Graphically think about and visualize the pain this action has caused you, referring to specific incidents and lost opportunities. Now write down your decision to dramatically improve and tape it to your bedside. Read it ten times before you go to bed and when you first wake up-it will slowly start to affect your subconscious mind which ultimately governs all of our actions.

Step 2: The Pattern Interrupt

Now that you are committed to the change, and maybe have told all your family and friends about it so that you have some positive pressure on you, you must start the re-conditioning process. When the first thought of the negative behaviour enters your mind, isolate it and interrupt the thinking process by anything unique: a silly sound that you make, a bizarre word like "ookabooka!", or a pinch to your leg. This may sound strange but it will have the highly important impact of breaking the disempowering thought pattern that is holding you back. Just as a person who walks in late at a presentation you are giving often interrupts your train of thought, you are training your mind to interrupt its limited thinking patterns.

Step 3: The New Reality

Once you have made the decision to change and interrupted the pattern, you must then replace it with the new behaviour you wish to cultivate. This is known as Opposition Thinking and is an ancient Indian technique practiced by the yogis who developed enormous mental powers. The essence of the strategy is to substitute the negative thought for a positive, empowering one. If you suffer from procrastination, each time the thought of wasting time while you should be working comes to your mind, isolate it, break the pattern and then substitute a clear thought of you working hard. Picture in your mind's eye the wonderful benefits of completing this task successfully. Will it increase your discipline and self-image? What positive effects will your new behaviour have this year if you keep doing it? How about in five or ten years. Start to Feelgood about this behaviour.

Step 4: Think Good Thoughts

Now that you have opposed the negative thought with the empowering one, it will slowly start to crumble as it realizes it is unwelcome in your winning mindset. Thoughts are things and it is so very important that you recognize that you control the thoughts in your mind -not the other way around. The key is to continually practice the process given to you above until the new, powerful thinking pattern is conditioned in your mind. Go over it and over it. Soon you will only think of the positive behaviour and it will become a habit. This is the first stage of your new destiny.

MEGATHINKING! & THE ENCHANTMENT OF POSITIVITY

Believe in yourself! Have faith in your abilities! Without a humble but reasonable confidence in your own powers you cannot be successful or happy.

Norman Vincent Peale

Program yourself for total success and self-confidence. What you think you will become. Your mind is the Universe's most powerful computer and you are the programmer. What you enter into it is all that will come out. The quality of your life therefore is a direct result of what you put into your mind -your programming. If you think negative thoughts all day, you will have little energy, no enthusiasm and may soon become ill. It is beyond debate in this age of mind-body medicine that thoughts are things that have a significant result on the physiology of the body. If you think weak thoughts, you are sending out bad signals to your body and filling it with harmful toxins that not only impede your performance but shorten your lifespan.

Megathinking! is a habit that you can cultivate. It is a mode of thinking without limitations. You see the wonders of life and the magic of your world. It is not seeing the world through rose-colored glasses and being unrealistic. It is seeing the cup half-full rather than half empty. It is recognizing that you can and deserve everything you want in this world and attaining your goals is simply a matter of believing in yourself and then taking tremendous action to accomplish them. A habit is like a wire cable. It starts off with a thin thread of wire and through constant conditioning, it becomes stronger and stronger until a time arrives when it cannot be broken. The MegaLiving! program will show you how to become a MegaThinker and see the immense possibilities that you may have been neglecting.

Olympic athletes have understood the tremendous power of the mind and the importance of mental discipline in sports excellence. At that level of competition, what separates the medal winners from the "also rans" is the "winner's mindset." Just as they enter into a top-flight conditioning program for their bodies, such athletes vigourously train their minds to focus on winning and peak performance.

The Champion's Mindset

Virtually every elite athlete now has a sports psychology regimen alongside nutritional considerations and general body training. Many say that the key is to harness the mind's incredible psychic energy to create the desired results. This can be done by visualizing success at the event, going through rituals in preparation for the event and practising meditation exercises designed to calm the body, ridding it of the stresses that hamper peak performance.

Increasingly, non-elite athletes and peak performers in the arena of life are applying the mental conditioning strategies of Olympians to live better, live longer and achieve more positive results. You must condition your mind and enter into a mind-training routine as if you were an elite athlete preparing for the event of your life. You must take your training seriously and become devoted to true excellence. You have phenomenal powers lurking deep inside of you, whether you realize this or not. You are likely only using 20% of your mind's vast reserves. What about the remaining 80%? If you want a supermemory, to have focus like a laserbeam, the creativity of a genius and the serenity of an Indian yogi living deep in the Himalayas, you must earn it and train your mind. This will not occur overnight but it *will* happen if you use your personal power to make it happen. The MegaLiving! 30 day program will get you on track for the big results that you want and deserve.

Also, it is imperative that you develop a winning attitude. You must *expect* to win at the game of life. Marcus Allen, the first-class NFL running back has said: "My whole game is attitude. You've got to think positively to achieve the impossible, to be what you expect to be. If you seek mediocrity, then that's all you get! " As you prepare for each day or a special event such as a big presentation, court case or sports meet, run a mental video of the perfect result in your mind. Smell the air, see all the details of the activity-the more precise the better. See yourself smiling and meeting with huge success. Think of how you want to feel and will feel. Feel the success and the pleasure you will receive on another job well done. Creative visualization works so

---

put it into your self-mastery arsenal.

Become the most positive person you know. Cultivate the spirit of positivity and joy in every area of your life. Become a true adventurer, seeing life's little obstacles as challenges that will allow you to become wiser and to grow. Learn to love adversity and to thrive on it. The great business leaders of our time from Getty to Ted Turner loved big challenges and turned them into opportunities for magnificent wealth. This is the difference between winners and losers. Losers see adversity as something that will break them and complain that life is hard. Winners design strategies to benefit from challenges, regroup if they do not work and maintain a burning commitment to succeed at all cost. Winners will always find a way.

THE MAGIC OF GOALS: YOUR VISIONS OF EXCELLENCE

Nothing can stop the man with the right mental attitude from achieving his goal; nothing on earth can help the man with the wrong mental attitude.

W.W. Ziege

Clear goals are the essential foundation of success and life mastery. Without clearly defined goals for both the near future and the long-term, you are like a ship moving through the deep seas without a course. Who knows where you may end up. Lasting self-mastery and life excellence will only come about when you set precise objectives for every facet of your life. Once you do this, your mind will spot opportunities to allow your desires to be filled and you will start to live your dreams.

One of the truest laws of Nature is that what you focus on constantly with great emotion and expectation will happen. You can use this age-old principle to destroy your life by thinking about the negatives or to make it phenomenal by aiming to the stars and expecting your desires to come true. As Henry Ford has said: "Thinking always ahead, thinking always of trying to do more, brings a state of mind in which nothing seems impossible." You do not start creating the life you want 20 years from now in 20 years, you start this very day by setting precise goals, developing a clear plan and then by taking massive action. Every day, you must take some action to advance you confidently in the direction of your ultimate destination. Every thought must be a useful one that will boost your enthusiasm for the accomplishment of your dreams. Step one on the magical road to success and a perfect life is the setting of your goals.

Here is the most effective strategy ever developed for achieving your goals:

1. **Know What You Want:** Find, recognize & mentally visualize the goals you are working towards. One of life's biggest success tips is to figure out what you love doing and then find someone who will pay you to do it. What are your secret ambitions? Perhaps the best way to determine your life goals is to write your own eulogy. Picture your own funeral and what you would like said about you and your accomplishments. Do you want to hear that you were the richest person in your country, the best piano player in your city or the happiest person that anyone had ever met? Think deeply about where you want to be in 5, 10 and 20 years. These are your life goals.

2. **Set Precise Goals with a Deadline**. Once you know the direction in which you are travelling through life, your days take on new meaning. You start to live with a tremendous passion and focus. The next step is to write out your goals very precisely (you will actually do this in the MegaLiving! Goal Setting Workshop which follows). Your goals must not only be clear but you must have specific time limits on the attainment of each one. This will put a little positive pressure on you to take real action every day.

3. **Let Your Goals Dominate Your Thoughts**. When one of the world's greatest scientists, Sir Isaac Newton, was asked the secret to his awesome success he replied that he thought of nothing else. Study any winner in life and you will see that they have trained their mind to think of nothing but the attainment of their goals. By thinking constantly of the

realization of their dreams, they develop a truly unshakeable belief and faith that every single one of their desires will come true. Winners expect success. Remember, that ageless principle: Your inner world determines your outer world. Therefore, every morning, recite your goals out loud. Take at least 10 minutes every evening and visualize yourself doing what you want to do. Picture the fun and happiness you will feel when, at the end of your life, you have done all that you wanted to do.

4. **Walk Before You Run.** There is no doubt that the only limitations to your life are those that you set. You truly can do anything. Having said this, you cannot sail around the world if you have never set foot on a boat. Identify the current obstacles to your dreams. List your weakness and what you plan to do to make improvements. What training will you need and who can you recruit to assist you. Set easily attainable goals at first. If your goals are too unrealistic early on, you may become discouraged when you really should not be. By meeting with little successes, your confidence and enthusiasm starts to explode and you can tackle your bigger challenges. Nothing can stop the person who refuses to be stopped!

5. **Success Has A Price.** Dreaming your dreams and expecting great results without taking any active steps to go forward is nothing more than unconstructive fantasizing. To unleash the incredible forces of your mind, you must pay a price and that price is action. You must give up any activities that are purely time wasting or bad habits that are standing as obstacles to your perfect life. The price you may have to pay is getting up earlier to review your goals or giving up watching television every night on the couch in favour of working on the brilliant business idea you have dreamed up. You must be willing to do whatever it takes to be a winner in life.

If it is peace of mind that you are ultimately searching for, you will have to find time to meditate and master your spiritual dimension. If it is perfect health, you will have to find time to develop your body, refine your diet and exercise. Whatever you are aiming towards, you must commit yourself to making small sacrifices for the larger good of your life goals. But once you are on the wonderful path of your goals, life changes very dramatically. You wake up with a fire in your belly and a passion for the day. You feel productive, confident and deeply happy. You feel fulfilled as if your life has true meaning. You become a creator, in full control of your destiny rather than a person who simply floats through life responding to whatever events fall into his path. With goals, you start to tap your human potential and realize the perfect life that has always been deep within you.

The Success Mechanism

In the early 1960's researchers learned that every person has a Success Mechanism built into their mind. This device works with your creative imagination and is goal striving. In other words, the Success Mechanism is triggered by positive goals that you give to it. Once you feed the mechanism a goal, it takes over and relies on all of your past experience to scan for any feedback and information which will allow it to accomplish the goal given. Ideas and inspirations that you may have been exposed to in the past almost unconsciously, are still deep inside of your mind, waiting to be recalled to assist you in your achievement. By setting clearly defined goals with time limits, your Success Mechanism leaps into action.

Hunches and intuition reflect nothing more than this tool at work. Most importantly, the mechanism is guided by the mental images of your past experiences. For example, if you were asked to give a big speech at the last convention you were at and fumbled badly, a mental picture of the event has been etched in your mind. You may have played and replayed the mental movie of the negative speech over and over in your mind until it became embedded in it. Now, when you have to give another speech, the mechanism scans for relevant information and comes up with this negative picture which often has the result of leading to another unsuccessful performance.

However, the Success Mechanism can be fooled. It cannot tell the difference between a mental picture that has actually happened (i.e., your bad speech) or one that you put into the mind by dreaming and visualizing. Therefore, by visualizing, over and over, yourself giving the perfect speech to thunderous applause and cheers, the mechanism picks up this "past experience" and powerfully ensures that it becomes a reality. Using this little-known knowledge, you can re-program your mind, which is really nothing more than the world's most powerful computer, by picturing in your mind's eye the achievement of each and every one of your goals. Be very graphic. If you desire a house in the Caribbean, see the style, color, location and dimensions. Feel how it would be to live in that house. Now determine what you must do to get the house. See the desired results happening and truly believe that they will be achieved. Practice this technique every day, whenever you have a quiet moment. This tool works and will bring you all that you desire. Can you really afford not to try it for at least 30 Days?

Earlier, it was strongly suggested that you "mirror image" someone who has met with an abundance of success in the field in which you are interested. When you do this, as well as when you study any great leader, businessperson or wonderperson, you will see that their mastery and results have arrived, in part, through the setting of clearly defined goals. Goals will serve to motivate, inspire and guide you as you reach for what you want out of life. Without them, you are gambling with your future. Do you really want to play the game of life as if it were a roulette wheel? Get some certainty into your life; set your goals!

Your Goal Setting Workshop!

Before moving on, please spend some time assessing your goals and aspirations. It is not only tremendously important to the success of the 30 day MegaLiving! program but it is a very fun exercise.

Step 1: Your Masterplan for Life Mastery

On a piece of paper, write out your mission statement in life. Make it succinct. Your mission statement is a capsule statement of what you want to have accomplished in your life and how you wish to be remembered. Keep it general but focused on the true keys of your life. It may read as follows:

> *My mission is to become a person of true character and integrity, contributing to my country and attaining a state of perfect health and mental serenity. I will have a superb family and professional life while I build lasting wealth. I will be courteous to all and live my life with tremendous zest and joy.*

This is your guiding light, a clear statement of where you are going in life. This masterplan will keep you on course when others try to push you off it or when life's wonderful obstacles visit you. Put it in a place where you can see it regularly such as beside your bathroom mirror and read it often.

Step 2: Your Personal Mastery Goals

Now that you know where you want to be at the end of your life in general terms, turn to specifics. Set the one year, five year and ten year goals for your personal development. Think of how fit you want to be, what personal qualities you wish to develop, what strategies you want to master, how you hope to feel, look and think, what kind of intellect and memory you want, what books, tapes and seminars do you desire to attend (the list goes on). Write them out as there is a dramatic impact on your subconscious mind when things are placed into writing. Very importantly, set time limits for yourself to achieve these results.

Top 10 Personal Mastery Goals for This Year & Time Limit

1. _____
2. _____
3. _____
4. _____
5. _____
6. _____
7. _____
8. _____
9. _____
10. _____

Throughout this book, it has been emphasized that there is no pursuit more noble than mastering yourself. Each day, it is crucial that you set aside some time to tend to yourself, to care for your mind, to relax your intellect and nurture your body and soul. Like everything else in this life, the key is to make the practice a habit if you truly want to be effective.

Now think about your life in five years. How do you want to feel? What do you want to know and what qualities do you desire to have. How about more passion for life, more joy, a better temperament, a greater degree of serenity and inner calmness, more enthusiasm and more creativity?

All these qualities can be yours if you start striving towards them today. Remember that you cannot start to design your future far off into the future. Jump start your life now with a wonderful set of challenges for yourself. All satisfaction in life comes from rising to the challenges you set for yourself and overcoming them with enthusiasm and vigor. Do not put off this exercise for even a day. It will change your life and set you on the path of personal mastery that you have always longed to walk.

Now list your top ten 5 year personal mastery goals:

Top Ten Personal Mastery Goals for Five Years

1. _____
2. _____
3. _____
4. _____
5. _____
6. _____
7. _____
8. _____
9. _____
10. _____

Top Ten Personal Mastery Goals for Ten Years

1. _____
2. _____
3. _____
4. _____
5. _____
6. _____
7. _____
8. _____
9. _____
10. _____

Step 3: Your Material & Fun Goals

At this stage of your goal setting workshop, you will think about and note down your material and fun goals. The only limits to what you can receive are those you *choose* to set up in your imagination. Let it run wild. There are many things that still remain mystical in this world and one of them is the principle of why when goals are written down and kept at the center of you mind, they come true provided you take action to have the desired result.

Do not analyze how Nature works. Simply think big and have some fun here. Note all the material things you want (be creative and precise). It is also essential that you write quickly and so that your true desires come out and so that you do not start to think your goals are too large to come true. Paupers have become millionaires in 12 months. No dream is ever too big. Do you want a house in Bermuda? How about scuba diving in the Cayman Islands or mountain climbing in Nepal. Do you want a BMW, a sailboat or a trip around the world? Write all these things down, quickly and with the time limits for their attainment. Start now!

Top Ten Material & Fun Goals for This Year

1._____
2._____
3._____
4._____
5._____
6._____
7._____
8._____
9._____
10._____

Top Ten Material & Fun Goals for Five Years

1._____
2._____
3._____
4._____
5._____
6._____
7._____
8._____
9._____
10._____

Top Ten Material & Fun Goals for Ten Years

1._____
2._____
3._____
4._____
5._____
6._____
7._____
8._____
9._____
10._____

Step 4: Your Financial Destiny

Meticulously consider where you want to be from a financial viewpoint over the next number of years. How much money do you want to make and by when? What amount would truly make you happy and allow you the freedom to do all the things you want to do? What investments do you want to own? Your financial destiny will affect your personal destiny so think about it very carefully.

Top Ten Financial Goals for This Year

1._____
2._____
3._____
4._____
5._____
6._____
7._____
8._____
9._____
10._____

Top Ten Financial Goals For Five Years

1._____
2._____
3._____
4._____
5._____
6._____
7._____
8._____
9._____
10._____

Top Ten Financial Goals For Ten Years

1._____
2._____
3._____
4._____
5._____
6._____
7._____
8._____
9._____
10._____

Goals are the lifeblood of lasting achievement and personal excellence. You have now set the goals that will provide you with inspiration and a burning desire. You now likely have the clearest picture you have ever had of your path of life and your true wants. Most people pass through life without any idea as to where they are going. You have now overcome this hurdle. The next key is to maintain a consistent focus on your goals. Never let these dreams die no matter how far off they might seem today. Nature works in fabulously wonderful ways. Once a goal is set and the mind concentrated on its achievement, Nature exerts its powerful influence to bring about its realization. Believe in your dreams, reach for the stars and have the destiny that you know is yours!

The Secret Success Formula

You have now completed your goal setting workshop. To assist you in achieving your goals quickly, the following **success formula** is offered:

1. *Clearly decide on your goal & picture its attainment in your mind*

2. *Develop a strong belief that it will come true by autosuggestion (repetition of the idea aloud) throughout the day*

3. *Through repetition of thought, the goal will become a burning desire*

4. *Develop a clear plan of how you will achieve the goal*

5. *Write out the goal, the plan of action & the date by which you will achieve it. Repeat this aloud 10 times a day with belief in its purpose and with intense feeling.*

This success formula may seem strange but it has been used by some of the world's most successful leaders and will work for you. Do not apply it for only a day and then give up. This is a special gift that you are receiving. Have faith in this formula and it will work wonders for you. All your dreams will be placed at the forefront of your consciousness and the forces of thought will make them come true.

Now that you know where you are going and you firmly believe that you will have all that you desire, you must regularly set aside some time (at least once every day) to review your goals and consider how you will feel once you reach them. By applying this strategy, you will constantly be motivating both your conscious and subconscious mind to fulfill your dreams.

As you move to higher levels in your life through the application of the powerful principles in the MegaLiving! program remember these words of Woodrow Wilson:

> We grow great by dreams. All big men are dreamers. They see things in the soft haze of a spring day or in the red fire of a long winter's evening. Some of us let great dreams die, but others nourish and protect them, nurse them through bad days till they bring them to the sunshine and light which comes always to those who sincerely hope that their dreams will come true.

> *If I have the belief that I can do it, I shall surely acquire the capacity to do it, even if I do not have it at the beginning.*
>
> *Mahatma Ghandi*

THE POWER OF EXERCISE: YOUR FOUNTAIN OF YOUTH

You can transform your life and lift it to a much higher level by one simple activity: exercise. People are willing to go under the knife to look years younger, try bizarre diets and coat their bodies with New Age longevity creams when everyone knows that the surefire way to look young and feel fantastic is to spend some time everyday in some form of physical activity.

Before his championship matches, chess superstar Bobby Fisher did not spend his days solely studying the chess strategies of his opponents nor practising this wonderfully intellectual game. He focused most of his training on becoming physically fit by running long distances and doing laps in the swimming pool to increase his physical stamina and mental endurance. This was his ultimate weapon to wear down his challengers and it should be yours.

Top executives, world leaders and other peak performers all have one thing in common: they have understood the tremendous powers of vigorous exercise on a daily basis as a tool for self-mastery and life excellence. Do not say that you are so busy you cannot afford to exercise. If you are truly busy, then you cannot afford not to exercise. Make one of the best decisions of your life and make that commitment to an exercise routine today. If you already are involved in a fitness program, take it to the next level or start competing in the sport of your interest. Remember the spirit of kaizen: if you are not moving forward, you are moving backward.

Here are just a few of the benefits you will receive from daily physical exercise:

a) *A significant increase in your energy levels/stamina*
b) *A higher state of general health*
c) *Better muscle tone and a trimmer physique*
d) *A much more relaxed and serene mental outlook*
e) *More enthusiasm and confidence*
f) *Greater alertness and mental poise*
g) *Less illness and enhanced achievement/productivity*
h) *More discipline in all areas of life*
i) *Increased circulation & oxygenation*
j) *Much greater resistance to stress*

Physical mastery will rocket you to a perfect life quicker than almost any other strategy. It is not expensive to achieve and can be exceptionally fun if you approach it with the right attitude. Once you are in a fitness program, you will become so used to it that it becomes a daily habit like brushing your teeth and showering. You do not think twice about these activities each day and the same approach must be taken to your exercise regimen. When you do, all aspects of your life will improve including your mental agility, social relationships and peace of mind. Sit down for a minute and write out five negative effects of not exercising that you truly want to avoid:

1.
2.
3.
4.
5.

Now consider 10 benefits you will receive from exercise, list the changes and impact it can have on your life both this year, in five years and in 20 years. *Really feel* what you will miss, what fun you will not enjoy if you do not wake up to the wonders of physical mastery.

<u>10 benefits that I will receive from exercise</u>

1._____

2._____

3._____

4._____

5._____

6._____

7._____

8._____

9._____

10._____

Now you have clarified in your mind the pain that you will suffer over the remaining years of your life without exercise and the big benefits you are bound to have if you make physical excellence a burning goal (The Feelgood Principle). The MegaLiving! 30 day program will provide you with the tools to unlock the perfect state of health that you are capable of achieving. But the first step to take is to make a commitment to physical mastery and a daily dose of exercise.

Here are just a few of the activities that will revitalize and juice-up your life:

* Running, walking or hiking in the mountains
* Swimming, playing tennis, weights or aerobics
* Having a brisk walk in natural surroundings
* Martial arts, yoga, deep breathing exercises
* Skating with your kids, rollerblading to work
* Gardening, running a marathon & cross-training
* Sailing, scuba diving or waterskiing
* Doing a mini-triathlon or jogging on the beach

If you are just getting into an exercise regimen, one of the best all-round pastimes for both body and mind conditioning is yoga. This centuries old activity will boost your stamina, provide you with exceptional relaxation and increase your concentration dramatically. Yoga, when combined with a healthful diet and positive thinking will have truly dramatic effects on your life and the passion that you bring to it. Try it a few times and you will never give it up.

Once you decide that you will accept the challenge of physical mastery, you must be disciplined, consistent and motivated in your workouts to see any real, lasting results. After about 30 days, things will really start to spark in all areas of your life and you will undoubtedly feel better than you have ever felt. In fact, you will feel unstoppable. Here are some tips to stay motivated:

1. Start off easy (15 min/day) and stay strong
2. Have fun and a positive, playful attitude
3. Get a partner with a similar goal of physical mastery
4. Cross-train with different sports to keep the regimen spicy
5. Write down your 1, 5 and 10 year fitness goals
6. Use positive motivators like pictures of what you will be
7. Use visualization techniques to focus on what you will be
8. Make the program a habit & do it at the same time daily
9. Affirm each minor success-the 1000 mile journey begins with one step
10. Use the momentum of daily minor successes from your program to catapult you to greater challenges: aim high!

Physical exercise will change you. It will add power and focus to your dreams. It is so simple. Out of the 168 hours in your week, can you not spare 6 or 7 in the interest of your longevity, mental toughness and happiness? You can. As stated by Humboldt: "True enjoyment comes from activity of the mind and exercise of the body; the two are ever united."

EATING YOUR WAY TO EXCELLENCE: MEGAFOOD NUTRITION

You are what you eat -nothing more and nothing less. By transforming your diet, you can dramatically reshape your body, moods, energy levels and overall vitality. All the mind conditioning strategies and self-mastery techniques discussed above will not help you if you do not have the energy and health to apply and excel with them. This section is about the fuels you put into your body, your physical miracle. By caring for it with proper and thoughtful nutrition, you will have the longevity and ability to have your dreams. By letting it fall apart and breakdown, your dreams will crumble and remain unfulfilled. The mind and body are powerfully linked and if one is not operating at its optimal level, the functioning of the other suffers. Treat both well and you create your magnificent destiny.

Eating Live Foods: A Giant Step to Physical Mastery!

The ancient yogis of India are an excellent study on longevity, physical mastery and mental toughness. Many live beyond the age of 100 and maintain a lithe, limber and strong body throughout their lives, being able to perform tremendous physical feats well into what North Americans consider their last years. What is their secret? It is simply that they, along with almost every other group known for exceptional longevity and good health, eat in moderation and follow a strictly natural diet.

The "sattvic" or pure diet is one based on living foods-those created by the natural interaction of the sun, air, soil and water. The "sattvic" diet emphasizes fruits (and their fresh juices), vegetables and grains. By making changes to your diet to ensure that these Megafoods form at least 70% of your diet, you will take the first step to ensuring physical mastery and a perfect life. Try it for 30 days only and you will surely be astonished by the phenomenal results. Here are some of the benefits you will receive when you start to eat living foods regularly rather than dead foods (meat products):

1.   A significant increase in your energy & stamina
2.   Enhanced concentration & creativity
3.   Decreased obesity, loss of body fat
4.   Enhanced complexion, skin tone and vitality
5.   Lower sleep requirements
6.   Less digestive difficulties
7.   Improved alertness & mental agility, memory
8.   A longer life with fewer diseases
9.   A greater sense of harmony with Nature
10.   General health excellence

A diet rich in vegetables, grains and fruits is truly what nature intended for us to have. For example, our teeth and intestines are strikingly different from carnivores such as dogs and are much more similar anatomically to fruit-eating primates. Meats such as beef and poultry are from dead beings and only provide second-hand nutrition -that gained from the animal eating natural fruits and vegetables. As well, animal flesh has been found to have a high proportion of toxins and lacks many of the important vitamins and minerals that we need to function at optimal levels. Importantly, meat is particularly hard to digest and greatly depletes our energy reserves in the digestive process. Natural foods such as fruits are easily digested, leaving the energy available for more productive pursuits like achieving your dreams and becoming the very best that you can be.

If meat is so bad for us, why do we eat it? Most proponents argue that vegetarian diets do not provide proper protein. But it is ironic that those who eat meat get the worst quality protein available. Meat protein contains too much uric acid to be broken down by the liver and can lead to serious health problems in later life. Vegetables and dairy products all provide an excellent source of protein and in a much higher quality than that found in meat products. One need only look at the most powerful animals on the planet. The elephant, rhino and gorilla (which has thirty times a man's strength) all survive on vegetables or fruits. Fruits and vegetables will provide you with all the building blocks for first-class protein.

Unlocking Your Energy Reserves : Exposing Your True Vitality

Energy is the essence of life excellence for without an abundance of it, you are like a rocket without fuel. For peak energy, it is important that you eat according to the natural cycles which occur in your body. They are as follows:

1.   **The Welcoming Cycle** (Megafoods such as fruits taken in and digested): *noon-8pm*

2.   **The Absorption Cycle** (the foods are used): *8pm-4am*

3.   **The Removal Cycle** (foods are eliminated): 4am-noon

By recognizing these natural body cycles and eating in a way to allow each cycle to be most effective, you will release your tremendous energy reserves and see more vibrant health than ever before. The key is to ensure that toxins are flushed out of the body and the body remains pure inside. This is done by considering the following:

1. *Eat high water content foods*

    70% of the planet is water as is 70% of our bodies. To properly cleanse your system and to ensure that it is in a peak performance state, you must make certain that your diet consists of at least 70% high water content foods (vegetables and fruits). The 3 body cycles function best when supplied with water from these sources on a regular basis (the 8 glasses of water a day theory floods the body).

2. *Work with the 3 Cycles*

    Once you are eating water-rich, live foods, you must ensure that your intake corresponds with the cycles. In the morning (until noon) when the body is trying to eliminate toxins and other wastes, eat only fruit. This will make the cleansing/elimination process *far* more efficient. After noon, have your meals (70% of your diet should be vegetables, grains and fruits). After 8pm, do not eat anything as this will hamper the absorption process and clog the system (again draining your energy reserves and working the digestive process overtime).

Making the nutritional changes above are not as difficult as they might seem. To ensure a high water content, simply have a salad with all your meals. In the morning (when you are eliminating wastes and should therefore only have fruit), start off the day powerfully with a glass of fresh orange or apple juice. One of the very best investments you can make is buying a juicer (now quite inexpensive). The are many excellent juicing books now on the market as juicing has become one of the hot trends across the country and combinations such as apple-strawberry and rasberry-watermelon should change the minds of even the most ardent non-believers.

For lunch, rather than a hot dog and fries, why not have a salad consisting of greens, peppers, artichokes, celery, carrots, green onion, marinated veggies and cherry tomatoes. You only need to visit one of the many wonderful salad bars in any office building to see that they are fabulously tasty and far different from the old, boring salads you may have had as a kid. For dinner, add meat if you must but make sure the meal is full of vegetables and grains to ensure optimal health and energy. Live this lifestyle for just one month and the transformation will blow your mind. This is not some trendy diet craze. This is for real. By eating natural, water-rich foods -Megafoods- you will be able to do all those things that you were always too tired to do. You will finally be able to have the fun you always wanted to have and, ultimately, live the life you have always wanted to live!

5 ANCIENT SECRETS OF LONGEVITY

Longevity Secret 1:   Breathing Your Way to Perfect Health

> *When the breath wanders, the mind is unsteady, but*
> *when the breath is still, so is the mind still.*
>
> *-ancient yoga principle*

Take food or water out of your life and you can live for days. Take away breath and you will die a quick death. Breathing is essential to living. Learn to breathe properly and you will not only develop the skill of changing your state of mind but you will dramatically enhance your energy levels. Good breathing practice fully oxygenates the body and charges up each and every one of your cells to fuel your activities and keep you in a state of high vitality. Good breathing practices will unleash the vitality that now lies inside you now waiting to be released. The techniques below are derived from age-old yogic practises and are now being recognized throughout the world as strategies for creating optimal health and happiness. Learn them, practise them and share them with others.

"To breathe properly is to live properly" said one ancient philosopher. Deep breathing will maintain a superb state of both mind and body fitness. It is now common to use deep breathing techniques to calm the mind when it is agitated or unfocused. Elite athletes do deep breathing exercises to fully relax and achieve peak performance at an important event. Actors and professional singers/speakers can be seen in the wings before a key performance tuning up their tools with deep breathing.

Proper breathing strategy is one of the most important elements of physical mastery and yet it is so very overlooked. Look back through the ages at activities such as yoga and the martial arts (which were created not only to build character but to maintain ideal health and longevity) and you will see that deep and proper breathing practices form the bedrock of these pursuits. If you want to live longer, be happier and think stronger, learn to breathe properly and practise the following exercises regularly.

Breathing Exercises for Perfect Health

1.   **Breathe & Hold: MegaBreathing!**

This technique, which will dramatically increase your energy after only a couple of weeks of steady practice, is simple to practice and can be done anywhere. It is also one of the very best exercises to improve your concentration if you are weak in this key area.

The essence of the exercise is to inhale to a count of two, hold your breath for a count of eight and exhale fully to the count of four. To aid you in your counting, you may use walking steps: walk for two steps while inhaling fresh air deep into your belly, hold for eight steps and exhale strongly for four more footsteps. You will soon notice the difference in your energy level and overall health levels.

2.   **Alternate Nostril Breathing**

This is a thousand year old technique currently being used by yoga teachers across North America to boost the energy levels of their students and produce a wide array of lasting benefits to the mind, body and spirit. After practising it, you will feel a mild feeling of euphoria.

Sit in a quiet area with your feet crossed and back straight. Place your right thumb over your right nostril and inhale (through your nose) to the count of two through your left nostril. Close your eyes when you do this and imagine a giant balloon expanding in your tummy when you take the inhalation. Now hold for the standard eight count and, at the same time cover your left nostril with your right pinky. Next, exhale to the count of four through your right nostril. At all times, your mouth should be closed. Next, your inhalation will be through the right nostril, hold and exhale through the left (your thumb is now on the right nostril). Practice this alternate nostril breathing for five minutes every morning and the benefits will come fast.

3.   **The Pump**

This is a quick energy booster which you may use before a big presentation or meeting. Simply sit down and place your hands over your belly as if you were cupping a balloon. Now pump/push in your stomach at the belly button area and exhale strongly through your nose at the same time. Then, inhale through your nose and push the belly outward. Repeat the process twenty times, speeding up as you grow more comfortable.

4.   **The Early Riser**

There is nothing quite as good for your mind, body and spirit than a beautiful walk through the woods or along the sea at 5 or 6 in the morning. Try it once a week, perhaps on Sunday mornings. It will calm your mind and allow you to maintain a balanced perspective on what this special life is really about and the wonders that are out there for the taking. Be sure to breathe deeply whilst you are walking (inhale two counts, hold eight, and exhale four).

5.   **Green Fog Breathing**

This is a technique developed by world-class martial artists to place them into a state of serenity and elevated calmness before competition.

The first principle of good breathing practice is to breathe with all of your lungs and not just from the top portion of them. Proper breathing occurs when you are using the top and bottom of the lungs, as you do naturally when you sleep.

Now lay down on your back in a place of quiet and shut your eyes. Repeat aloud the following phrase slowly: "I am serene, strong and focused." Then while you inhale, visualize the air as deep green fog entering your body through your nostrils, moving slowly into the depths of your abdomen. The green fog then moves through the limbs and throughout the body. Next, when the calming green fog has travelled through the body relaxing every muscle, exhale it along with any tensions that may have accumulated.

Keep doing this deep breathing exercise for 5 -20 minutes daily (preferably first thing in the morning or before any stressful situations for immediate calmness and internal peace). Deep breathing can change the state of your mind & your life.

The above breathing exercises reflect the very best breathing conditioners for the mind, body and spirit. You can take your general health to a far higher level simply by applying the above techniques on a daily basis for thirty days. You only need to spend 10 or 15 minutes a day on the strategies but you will surely reap huge gains and carry out all the important tasks that you do with improved vigor and enthusiasm. With the greater energy reserve deep breathing generates, you can do more, achieve more and transform your world from the commonplace to the ideal.

Longevity Secret 2:   **The Importance of Proper Chewing**

It has been explained earlier that the process of digestion is extremely energy consuming and the easier the process is made, the more energy will be available to you for other pursuits. Proper and slow chewing of all food might sound like an immaterial activity but it is essential for perfect health and youthful vigor.

Most people are in such a hurry, they gobble down food, half chewed. Food should be digested in the mouth before being digested in the stomach. Otherwise the food sits in the stomach for long periods when, had it been chewed properly by the teeth, it would have moved along nicely and been absorbed by the body.

Properly chewed food is digested much easier which also means that your body requires less of it. So with proper chewing, you can cut down on your intake and still be far healthier than you ever were. People in our society eat far more than they require anyway and it is a sound principle of longevity to eat better food in lesser quantities rather that more food, poor in quality. As said by Benjamin Franklin: "To lengthen thy life, lessen thy meals."

Longevity Secret 3:   **Stop Acting Old**

Jean Jacques Rousseau wrote "a feeble body enfeebles the mind." To achieve perfect health and start MegaLiving! you must not let an old person move into your body. Guard against acting old and the habits of old people. Maintaining a youthful lifestyle will keep you young.

Also, do not let your posture go to ruins. Keep your back straight and your head held high. Walk with purposeful steps in a smooth strong cadence. An excellent posture is something you must always be aware of and is really a habit to be formed. The health benefits of good posture, and the excellent breathing it allows, are very dramatic.

Another useful tip is to see yourself as a person in peak health. Two or three

---

times a day, shut your eyes and picture clearly the person you want to become physically. See the brilliant glow in your face and eyes and notice the smooth tone of your skin and muscles. See yourself laughing and feel the energy that you have cultivated. By now you are an expert at making mental pictures and must realize the incredible power this technique offers. Make such pictures for only a month and you will notice a huge difference. Your self-image will have improved, you will feel better and you will have more enthusiasm for carrying out the routines that will put you on the road to physical mastery.

Anything that you want to be, you can be if you hold a clear picture of the desired goal in your mind with deep conviction and emotion that it will become a reality. Add to the mix a definite timeframe for the achievement of the goal, a clear plan and daily steps in the direction of your dream and you truly become unstoppable! Do not give up. You are a person of great character and courage, only the weak fail and never climb the mountain of life mastery and Perfect Health. And not only is this journey to the higher reaches of your life a spectacular adventure but the ultimate destination is clearly within your grasp.

Longevity Secret 4: The Outstanding Benefits of Yoga

One of the easiest strategies for powerful physical and mental transformation is yoga. Designed thousands of years ago by the wisemen of India as a total means of achieving and maintaining perfect health of the mind, body and spirit, it will do wonders for you. The essence of yoga is that through a number of physical exercises (asanas), general relaxation techniques, a lighter diet (satvic), good breathing practice and positive thinking, a person can elevate his condition to one of real excellence where the mind and body become one for lasting good health.

Hatha Yoga programs are offered throughout North America and Europe at inexpensive rates. The programs are relaxing and very enjoyable. As well, the ideas and exercises are easy to learn when guided by a well-trained teacher. If you have yet to try yoga, you are missing out on one of the very best health tonics and elixirs for youth.

> *If one advances confidently in the direction of his own dreams, and*
> *endeavors to live the life which he has imagined, he will meet with*
> *a success unexpected in common hours.*
>
> *Thoreau*

You have the potential to create a new reality beginning today. This new reality can be one of perfect health, abundant wealth and absolute bliss. You too can meet with a success unexpected in common hours. The preceding pages have provided you with numerous strategies for mastering your mind and body. Precise exercises and powerful routines appear in the 30 day MegaLiving! program which follows at the end of this book. But through all the principles, through all the meditations and techniques, one burning truth stands out above all the rest. That truth is the most potent secret of longevity, peak health and life mastery.

That truth is simply stated: *your thoughts control your world*. If you firmly stand guard at the door of your mind and let only the very best thoughts enter, you will be happy, healthy and serene. If you let thoughts of negative past and future experiences dominate your mind, you will meet with them, you will never enjoy bliss and you will not even come close to the state known as perfect health. Be a firm guardian of each and every thought and idea that enters your mind and make certain it is of the highest quality.

As an avid gardener tends daily to her garden, nurturing it with all that is good, you must nurture and cultivate your mind. If you do this and zealously guard against the weeds which will attempt to take root by thinking positive, inspiring thoughts only, you will see great things blossom. Everything is created twice-first in your mind and then in the outside world. Just as a builder first drafts a building on paper before he starts to build it, you must create all that you desire in your mind's eye. If you do this, if you dream great dreams and good thoughts, forces which you will never understand will be activated to bring you to your goals.

Change your thoughts and you will radically alter your life. Think of perfect health and you will undoubtedly have it. See yourself as a confident, strong and passionate person within your imagination and you will soon transform into this vision. See yourself as a wealthy person, think this thought for twenty or thirty minutes daily with true belief in its attainment and you will have it.

Thoughts combined with the emotion of faith and belief yield phenomenal results. If you wish to perfect your body, first perfect your mind. Be a strong warrior, determined to think happy, wonderful thoughts only. Slay any thought that is not powerful and conducive to the mindset of a winner at life's game. You are the master of your thoughts. The sooner you realize this as well as the control that we have all been given over our thinking process, the sooner you will see real and lasting self-mastery. You are responsible for your thoughts. With practice and discipline, you will reign supreme over each and every thought in your mind. You will then create a personal destiny second to none.

As stated by James Allen in the excellent little book, *As a Man Thinketh* : "As the physically weak man can make himself strong by careful and patient training, so the man of weak thoughts can make them strong by exercising himself in right thinking." So what is the secret of longevity and personal excellence? Master your thoughts and you will master your mind; master your mind and you will master your body; master your body and you will feel as you have never felt before- you will feel perfect health.

The ancient thinkers arrived at the conclusion that thoughts are things and, like every other thing in this world, they are made up of energy. So with every thought, you have actually created something. You have sent a mental messenger from your mind out into the world. And this messenger, if it is of the correct nature, will influence all aspects of your material life as the energy of the thought influences the energy of all matter. Positive thinking is not some abstract concept but is, rather, grounded in the physical principles of the world. Thought is matter and thoughts influence matter. This is why belief in your desires and goals is so very powerful and can reshape your life.

Miracles happen every day. Cancer patients have reportedly been cured by a diet of positive thinking after traditional medical treatments have failed. People who have had nothing have pulled themselves up to greatness by making a decision to make their lives better and then taking action to ensure that this happened. Is there any doubt that in your mind, you hold the most incredible instrument of change and success ever created?

The MegaLiving! 30 Day Program will show you how to run and further condition your mind. It is the ultimate owner's manual for your greatest asset. If you commit yourself to the simple exercises given to you, you will take the most important step of your life, the first step to mastering your mind and, thus, your world.

> *Everyone knows that weeds eat out the life of the garden and of the productive fields. The gardener and the farmer alike each has to keep the weeding process alive... It's like that in the building and developing of character. No one knows our faults and tendencies better than we do ourselves, so that it is up to each one of us to keep the weeds out, and to keep all growth vigorous and fruitful.*
>
> George Matthew Adams

Before you can ever hope to change your circumstances, you must first improve yourself. The starting point, as always, is with your thoughts. The surface of your thoughts is your character. All of the thoughts which dominate your mind, come together like the wires of a powerful cable to create your character. If you have weak thoughts, you will most certainly have a weak character. Be a strongly disciplined thinker and you are assured of a strong, unstoppable character.

THE PLEASURES OF PROACTIVITY

You are responsible for everything that happens to you in your life. You can make your existence a shining example of personal and professional excellence or you can make your life a living hell. The key is really to realize that you have the power to see problems as challenges and to take any action required to have what you want. The quality of your life is determined by your interpretation of what happens to you.

Being proactive means you no longer chalk up past failures or lack of achievement to your family background or personal circumstances. Being proactive means that you no longer cry over spilt milk and complain about the hand this world has dealt you. You are "pro-active": for action.

You must exercise your proactivity muscles to develop the mindset of a true champion. You must see yourself as a little god on this earth, one who has all the qualities required for great success and a burning desire to achieve it. If you have such dreams, you will indeed find a way to achieve them. Ghandi, Ford, Lincon, Bell, Kennedy and Salk all did and so can you.

Once you develop the magical habit of thinking without limits, a new reality will unfold. When you begin to realize that you hold in your mind infinite power to shape your destiny, wonderful things start to happen. More than likely, you are only using 20% of your mind's incredible potential. What about the rest? Are you really willing to waste the billions of brain cells that you have been given and the marvel we call the human body on a life of mediocrity? This book is your wake up call. In the twinkling of an eye, this very second you can transform your life. Make the decision and the commitment to be the very best you can be.

Being proactive means you shape circumstances and they do not shape you. You have the choice of interpreting any event that has happened in the past or that will unfold in the future according to *your* wishes. For example, if someone is particularly insulting to you, you have a choice as to how you interpret the event. The average person becomes angry and repeatedly asks himself why someone would do this to him-pushing himself into a negative, fully unproductive state. The person who has developed proactivity appreciates that he has the power to interpret the event in a manner to empower him. The key is the interpretation of the action and to choose to see the event as one that will help you grow. You may make the following interpretations from an otherwise negative circumstance of someone being rude to you:

i)   Poor fellow, what can I do to help him-he must be having a bad day.
ii) How can I learn from this event and use it as a growth experience on my path to life mastery?
iii) Everything happens for a reason and something positive will come out of this situation.
iv) What will happen to me (both physically and mentally) if I let this minor incident bother me? Am I majoring in minor things?

v)   I must see myself as an orange-when squeezed, only what is inside will
      come out. If I have truly cultivated serenity, kindness and self-control,
      only these wonderful qualities will appear. If negative qualities come
      out, I still have some work to do on my journey to personal
      mastery.

Remember, it is not the snake bite that kills but the venom which circulates
afterwards that is fatal. Do not let the snakebite of another person release any
venom inside of you. You can control its entry and you are responsible for
every thought in your mind. You can make every day a living masterpiece.

Being proactive means that you can live a blissful existence, seeing the good
in all events unfolding on the beautiful canopy of life. There is no such thing
as an unpleasant experience. Every experience has the potential to improve
an element of your character or to present a challenge to you which may lift
you to a higher level spiritually, physically, mentally and professionally.
True winners see problems as great opportunities. Where others fail, they
thrive. In any recession, there are always a handful of entrepreneurs who
make their fortune, the stock players who are buying when everyone else is
selling. See the blue sky in every rain storm-it is there.

Proactivity is the first step to personal mastery. It is really nothing more than
self-control. And self-control, like all essential mastery qualities, can be
developed through patient and consistent perseverance and regular
exercising. Once you make the choice to run these muscles on a daily basis,
you will take real control of your life and awaken the true potential that now
slumbers deep within you. Will you accept the challenge?

MOMENTUM ON THE PATH TO MASTERY

There is a magic in momentum. As a jet accelerating down a runway increases its momentum before it finally takes off into the deep blue sky, you can use the momentum created by little self mastery successes to guide you to your ultimate goal of a perfect life.

This is the essence of the MegaLiving! 30 Day Program. Start off small with minor changes in your mental attitude, in your exercise program, in your diet and in your life habits. Soon the steps taken grow larger and the results more tangible until you are finally unstoppable. The journey of a thousand miles begins with a single step and you must start off small if you want to see big results.

In the area of your mental development, you will start enriching your mind's diet with excellent motivational books, positive, inspirational thoughts and exercises to improve your mental agility and stamina. At first, you will only be spending a few minutes a day on this but once you see the dramatic results which appear, you will become more devoted to realizing the potential of your intellect. Throughout this book, it has been emphasized that your mind is like any of the other muscles of the body: you must use it or "lose it". Not only must you use it, but if you do not push it and challenge it daily, it will grow weaker.

If you are not going forward, you are going backward. And if you constantly feed your mind with wonderful treats and condition it for excellence, you will certainly meet with success and happiness not expected in common hours. It does not matter if you have had a poor memory in the past or if you have been a negative thinker all of your life. You can change your focus and your beliefs with a simple commitment to change and a daily dose of mental practice for at least 30 days (and then maintaining your gains by daily conditioning). Nothing is more noble in this life than enhancing your mind and developing your character. Such actions will dramatically improve the quality of your life and the lives of those that surround you.

The same momentum that will propel your mindset to its highest levels will take you to physical mastery. You have a deep fountain of perfect health sleeping serenely inside of you. You must tap into this ocean of peak health and allow it to express itself. This is exceptionally important and you must realize the body's real potential for physical excellence.

The very best physician is a mind full of good thoughts, thoughts of hope, courage, strength and bliss. By feeding your body an equivalent diet of high water content foods (fruits & vegetables) and other healthful choices, it will regain the youthful form it may have lost and give you the energy you may have been lacking with a poor, hard to digest diet. By making small but significant changes in your diet, you will soon develop an incredible momentum that will build Habits of Health.

These habits will provide you with the discipline to eat well for the rest of your life- giving you a better body, better general health and the motivation to be the very best you can be. Tap into your reservoir of perfect health and start yourself on the course of MegaLiving! You will never turn back once you see the results of which you are truly capable.

A MISSION STATEMENT: YOUR LIFE PLAN FOR SELF-MASTERY

Without a concrete life plan & precisely defined goals, you are like a ship drifting aimlessly in the sea. You will go wherever the tide decides to take you. Such a lifestyle is not only one which leads to little productivity and personal effectiveness but one which provides no happiness and no fulfillment.

To meet with any lasting success and life mastery, you must chart your course in advance, planning for the achievement of your dreams and preparing to deal with the wonderful curves that life deals along the way. It is essential that you take the time to deeply think about what you want to hear at your testimonial dinner that was discussed at the opening of this book and determine what meaning you hope to attach to your life.

Many powerful strategies for goal fulfillment were explained to you in the Goal Setting Workshop contained earlier in this book. But every person truly interested in getting the very most out of life must take the time to develop a definite mission statement. A mission statement, vital for real self-mastery, is nothing more than a capsule statement of your life's purpose and objectives. It must come from your deepest core and reflect the fundamental principles which drive you. It must inspire you and accurately represent your dreams, ideals and desires.

With a mission statement in place, the meaning of your life and the course of your life's path is set (although this does not mean that your mission cannot change as you develop and progress through life). With a clear idea of what you want out of life and the guiding principles by which you will live, your world becomes filled with a tremendous sense of security and confidence. When opportunities and challenges present themselves, you can meet them easily because you are certain of the direction in which you are travelling and the ultimate destination. You simply select that course of action which will take you where you want to go. Much like the salesman who will get a large bonus if he meets his target of selling 1000 units of his product concentrates primarily on only those activities which will lead him to his goal, a mission statement concentrates your mind on those actions which are most important to success in your life.

A mission statement allows you to live with greater integrity and acts as a powerful compass to keep your life pointed towards your values. If someone suggests you do something contrary to your mission, you can immediately recognize this and refuse the suggestion. If part of your mission statement is to always act with kindness and courtesy because this is the kind of person you aspire to be known as, when someone treats you harshly, you will never respond in kind because it would go against the core values in your mission. You then remove regret from your world because you start to act the way you really want to act and others cannot cause a response that you dislike. You become proactive rather than reactive. You take charge and complete control over your life. You become principle centered, living in a way consistent with your fundamental values.

Here are a few of the benefits of a mission statement for your life:

i)   *Clarification of the purpose of your life and its guiding values*

ii)   *A mission will offer you a constant source of guidance in times of difficulty or challenge.*

iii)   *It will keep you motivated and act as a compass, pointing you at all times to the True North principles which you value most.*

iv)   *It will give you a much better sense of balance and allow you to define your life's priorities.*

v)   *It will help you to manage your time much better, placing emphasis on those activities that will yield the greatest results (80% of life's real accomplishments come from only 20% of your activities so put first things first).*

A mission statement is really nothing more than a few paragraphs or pages setting out what your life is about. It should say in general terms what are the key roles in your life and what you will achieve at the end of your existence. It should also set out those values that mean most to you and the qualities you aspire to having.

Develop your mission statement and foster your burning desire to soar to success. Today and every day that follows, you can tap the magical source of mastery that is your true potential. Today is the day you start being far more than you have been in the past. Today you start MegaLiving!

HOW TO ATTRACT WEALTH

Wealth means many things to many people. To a person in the world of business, it might mean a net worth of $50,000,000. To a person more focused on the spiritual aspects of life, it may mean the attainment of peace of mind and a deep faith in the existence and powers of a divine being. Most people are searching for some sort of wealth in their lives and what follows are the time-tested secrets of achieving it.

The first step to the realization of lasting wealth is to know what wealth means to you. What is it that you are searching for? Remember that happiness is not a destination but a way of travelling through life's journey. Happiness is not an oasis that lies at the edge of the desert, a place that you reach only when you are prosperous. Study many of the greatest success stories of our time and they will say that they were happiest when they were starting to build their massive fortunes. They were happiest when they were working against the odds and had the raging fire of ambition and determination burning in their bellies. Determine to be happy now, not later. This requires nothing more than a conscious choice on your part.

Once you have figured out very clearly what wealth means to you and what your key destination is, the next step is to develop what is known as a prosperity consciousness. To be wealthy, you must think wealthy. As with all success, everything begins with the mind since your outer world reflects your inner world. Recognize that the mind is a treasure house of power to bring you all the richness you seek. It will soon come as surely as the night follows the day.

Every man and woman in this world was born to succeed, be wealthy and be prosperous. The potential for prosperity is one of your most essential human qualities, whether you realize it or not. If there is not an abundance of all that you desire in your life, do something about it and do something this very day. It all begins by tapping the hidden and magical powers of that part of your mind that you may not even know exists: your subconscious mind.

The subconscious mind, containing infinite wisdom and capability, is brought to life through your beliefs. It responds to suggestion, both verbal (autosuggestion) and mental (through the form of pictures in your mind's eye). By repetition of phrases directed to the importance of prosperity in your life, you will soon enter a wealthy state of mind. This state of mind was the guiding force of every superachiever before you.

The beliefs which you hold in this mindset are then impressed on the subconscious mind which brings forth an abundance of opportunities for lasting wealth to become your reality. The key is to let your beliefs and faith in the fact that you will one day grow very rich penetrate your emotions. To become wealthy, you must feel wealthy. You must emotionalize your commitment to prosperity and let every thought you put in your mind dwell on this essential outcome. When you soak your mind in thoughts of wealth, happiness and peace, you start to tap and harness the incredible power of the subconscious mind. It is at this point that your life rises above the ordinary to the realm of the extraordinary, where it truly belongs.

For hundreds of years, great success stories have learned to concentrate the limitless power of the subconscious mind which many claim is the direct link to divine power beyond this material world. Whether you subscribe to this philosophy or not, it is essential to your prosperity that you realize that your subconscious mind can do wonders for you when you feed it the right nutrition in the form of affirmations (autosuggestion) and mental pictures (visualization).

Here is the best strategy for using your subconscious mind to achieve your dreams:

1. Get into a very relaxed state using one of the techniques you have learned in this book.

2. Mentally picture, in tremendous detail what it is you want (10 min.)

3. Tell yourself, out loud what you desire & that the result will come.

When you get into a truly relaxed, serene state, the subconscious part of the mind is most receptive to your suggestion. It will act on your every wish and make things happen. The essential key is to condition it just as you condition your subconscious mind for happiness by filling it with only the very best mental food.

Create your own personal mantras to repeat over and over to your subconscious mind when it is in this Ideal Action State of perfect relaxation. Load up your mind with vivid pictures of what you will look like when you are prosperous. How will you feel? What will your house, car and family look like? See the many zeroes after the number one in your bank book. Get emotional. What emotions will flood through you when you are wealthy? How will you feel about yourself?

In doing this exercise, every single day, you are simply applying one of the least known but most powerful of the laws of Nature: The Law of Attraction. This law states that what you constantly and consistently focus on in your inner world is precisely what you will receive in your outer world. As you sow in the wonderful garden of the mind, so shall you reap. Whatever you believe as true in your mind's eye will certainly manifest itself in your reality. As Emerson has said: "A man is what he thinks all day long." Understand this concept and you become unstoppable.

If you do not have all that you want in life, today is the day to start the reconditioning process. You are developing that state of magical thinking known as prosperity consciousness. Soon, you will start attracting tremendous opportunities and gifts that you never thought possible. The more you focus on your wishes, the more you believe deeply in their realization and the more every thought in your mind is a good one, the more you will receive. Throughout the day, affirm "I am attracting great prosperity and wealth." Also repeat, "every day in every single way, I am getting better and better." Never let go of the tight hold on your dreams. They will all come about. But first, once and for all, agree that the mind is the source of unlimited power.

THE LOST ART OF EFFECTIVE PERSONAL MANAGEMENT

Before you can do wonders in the outside world, you must first raise your standards about what you can do in your inner world. The essence of effective personal management is effective mind management. And the essence of effective mind management is mental discipline which is nothing more that controlling each and every thought to ensure that it is a useful and good one. Every thought concentrated in the direction of your dreams is like a little nugget of gold, advancing you confidently in the direction of lasting life wealth.

When your every thought is in the direction of where you want to go in your life, that is in the direction written clearly in your mission statement, your actions follow and become productive ones. Everything is created twice: once as a blueprint in the mind's eye and later in your reality. The process is very similar to the work of an architect who first drafts a sketch and plan of the way things will look in the new building and then methodically follows this blueprint to create the structure.

The guiding principle in effective personal management is a simple one: put your life goals first. By your mission statement, you know very precisely what matters most to you. It may be becoming the very best family man that you can be or the kindest mother ever to walk the face of this earth. Your life's goals may be to become incredibly rich or famous. Perhaps you have determined that you want to be a doctor or a professional athlete. Part of your mission may be to develop your character to the fullest or get into super shape and create a winner's mindset. Your mission might also include the goal of achieving peace of mind and inner serenity. Any of these dreams are attainable, you have learned that. The key now is to see that every thought and action taken in the direction of these goals will get you closer to them. Remember the 80/20 Rule: 80% of the results come from 20% of your activities. Recognize which activities will make the difference in your life and get you to where you want to go. Then focus your energy and attention on these. This is one of the best Secrets of Successful Living.

Every step in another direction, no matter how pleasant it might be, will keep you that much farther from what you have already determined means most to you in your life. Therefore, the overriding principle is to never let what matters most to you be sacrificed to those things that matter the least.

Your time and daily activities all exist within the three points of the Triangle of Personal Management. As you will see in the diagram which follows, your actions fall somewhere within Segments 1, 2 or 3 (S1, S2 or S3) and the Heart of the Triangle. S1 reflects activities which you might be doing which are pleasurable but of no value (i.e., television often falls into this segment of the triangle; you enjoy watching it but recognize it really gets you nowhere). S2 reflects those activities which appear productive and important but which really have little "Big Picture" value because they do not advance your mission and life goals. For example, you might spend a lot of time over a year learning to be an expert in computers but it is really time wasted if your life's primary goal is to be a concert pianist and a first class amateur athlete. S3 reflects those crisis activities that always require our attention whether we like it or not. These are the little brush fires and urgent matters which often appear as we journey through life and take up an undue amount of our energy.

In the center of the Triangle of Personal Management is the Heart of the Triangle. When you have thought deeply about what you truly want out of your life, when you know what your life's mission and meaning is, this place will be your home. When every thought is in the direction of your goals and dreams, almost every second of your time will be spent in the heart of the Triangle. And when it is, your life will take on enormous power. You will become the strong master of your mind, your body and your character. You will start to realize that nothing is impossible and that your dreams are not beyond your grasp. You will reach this level of thinking and you will visit this place very soon if you stay committed, enthusiastic and concentrated on the limitless possibilities of your life. This is not a place for a select few people. This is a place where you belong with all others who raise their lives beyond the mundane to the infinite. This is a place where hopes and desires all come true. This is the place of MegaLiving!

Study the Triangle of Personal Management and commit yourself to living your life within the Heart of the Triangle. This will not be a restricting way to live but a very freeing way of organizing your life according to your dreams and guiding principles. You start to develop unshakeable confidence and security as well as an appreciation for the value of time and the limitless achievement which is your potential.

The Triangle of Personal Management

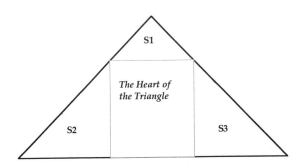

Living your life according to the Triangle of Personal Management is not just one way to live, it is the only way to organize your life. If you study every great superachiever, if you study anyone who has arrived at their Perfect Life, you will see that they live by the Triangle.

It is essential to live a life of balance. Thousands of years ago, in ancient India, it was written in the Bhagavad Gita that one should never live a life of extremes. Every person must strive for a balance between moderation and the burning desire to fulfill one's potential. By living with both eyes firmly planted in the direction of your goals, you do not lose the balance and fun that this world has to offer. First, there is nothing more fun than attaining your goals. Second, your life goals (your mission) must be sufficiently thought out to maintain the essential balance in life. For example, your mission statement should include life goals such as being the most adventurous person you know or the most balanced, relaxed person anywhere. A good mission will keep you on track but also well-rounded.

THE PATH OF THE MASTER

We live in a "quick-fix" society. We want everything in a flash. Faxes send information across the world in a matter of seconds and computers can tap the knowledge of the ages with a couple of keystrokes. We want fast food, fast service and fast learning. But some things do take time, disciplined effort and hard work. You have taken the time to get this far in the book. You have sacrificed other things to commit yourself to being the very best you can be by studying the strategies of MegaLiving! Part II will reveal to you the 200 MasterSecrets to Success while Part III contains the revolutionary 30 Day Program to self-mastery and a Perfect Life. But before you move on to the next part, please consider what mastery is all about.

What is mastery? Mastery is nothing more than a state of performance one reaches where every action in the mastered activity reflects unconscious excellence. Think of the martial arts master who has achieved a 5th degree black belt. He no longer has to think about each of the movements he must take to strike a blow or execute a kick through a wooden board. When this master throws a punch, he does not think to himself "first I must raise my arm, then I must pull it back and finally I must release it with tremendous force to strike at my intended target." Rather, after many hundreds of days of consistent and concentrated practice, he has reached a level of performance where a punch can fly as easily as the master can breathe.

The same is true for the concert pianist, the elite athlete or the top flight trial lawyer who, once on his feet in the courtroom, enters a zone or mental state where every ounce of focus is on the case before the judge. Nothing else matters and time has no meaning. The true master, when engaged in the mastered activity, lives purely in the moment. You have had such experiences. Think of the times when you played sports and were in a very challenging game. Nothing else was on your mind and nothing else mattered. Hours passed by like minutes and you experienced true Bliss and joy.

"A man possesses nothing certainly save a brief loan of his own body yet the body of man is capable of much curious pleasure," wrote J.B. Cabell. We are capable of incredible pleasure and happiness in our lives. The state of the true master, where time slips merrily by while the activity is being performed, has been called the state of Flow and can be cultivated. Just as the karate master enters this ideal performance state during his practice or competition, you can tap Flow in your daily life after you have mastered your mind, body and spirit. Flow is nothing more than the ideal state of concentrated attention but it provides an almost magical feeling.

Mastery and the state of Flow intersect at the point of living in the moment. All masters live in the moment and all individuals who have mastered their lives enjoy Flow. What all of these people have in common is the skill of making every moment count and thinking only of what matters most in their lives in every minute to the exclusion of other less productive, trivial thoughts.

The young woman who grew up in poverty dreams of one day becoming the world's best eye surgeon. When she concentrates her attention on this goal with the force of a laserbeam, not only does she set into play incredible forces which start moving to bring about her desire, she also starts to live in each moment and with true happiness. Her mind is on what she wants. She thinks of little else and her activities are the result of a strong mind with its attention in the correct direction.

This woman's energies are not dissipated by worry or by other life sucking mental diseases that distract the average person from living up to their real potential. This woman understands the laws of nature and knows the nature of the mind. She knows that her mind, with its goal seeking Success Mechanism, will do what she has instructed it to do. She now sets about to take massive action to get what she wants with faith in its attainment. This woman has set about on the path of mastery and will start to experience Flow on a regular, if not daily basis. She will start to experience Bliss and deep peace. She starts to realize that her life is indeed a Perfect one.

The path of mastery rises above the world of the "quick-fix." Mastery of your mind, body and character, just like mastery of any other activity, requires discipline, persistence and hard work. But the results will change every element of your life and you will understand that there truly is no more noble cause than strengthening yourself.

The 8 Keys to the Path of Mastery

The First Key to Mastery: Commitment & Desire

As with every important goal, it is essential to know your outcome and precisely what you want. Sit down and assess your desire. Is it a worthy, productive one? What benefits will you receive through mastery of the activity in question? Then make a decision to reach the point of mastery. Make a pact with yourself to do whatever it takes to get to your goal. Think how you will feel as a master of the desired activity. Think about the confidence that this will inspire in you. You are a person of character, push yourself to achieve what you want.

The Second Key to Mastery: Knowledge & Instruction

Once you are certain of your outcome, become determined to amass a storehouse of knowledge on the subject you want to master. The answers to everything you would ever want to know are out there. All of life's mistakes have already been made. Is there really a need for you to make them all over again?

Talk to people who have become masters. What did they do to achieve their success? Read books on the subject, listen to cassettes and go to seminars to understand what it is you must do to advance on your chosen path of mastery. Seek out the very best instruction possible and listen to what you are taught. Learn to associate a tremendous amount of pleasure with learning. You will never be disappointed and your life will become one inspiring adventure.

The Third Key to Mastery: Kaizen & Consistent Practice

You have learned about the wonders of Kaizen, constant and never-ending improvement, in an earlier section.   To gain total mastery of yourself, you must do something every single day to develop yourself and your potential. This is nothing more than practice and the development of good habits which will help you reach the higher levels you aspire to.

A martial arts student must practice regularly if he wants to receive a black belt.   At first the workouts are hard and seem like nothing more than drudgery. The student asks himself, "why am I putting myself through this?" After about three weeks of practice, the student notices transformations. The workouts start to get easier, he starts to develop more stamina and endurance and his technique starts to look pretty good. Soon his confidence increases and he starts to have fun with the activity. The student is now on the path of mastery and, in time, will definitely get there.

Any changes in one's life habits cause discomfort at first.   Exercising, meditation or the daily habit of filling your mind with some new ideas for personal growth might be hard at first. But every time you push yourself past any obstacles, you make yourself that much stronger. The next time is always a little easier.

The Fourth Key to Mastery: Persistence

No path is free of challenges and obstacles. This is the way of Nature. Little hurdles appear to offer you tests and opportunities to refine and expand yourself even further.   Think of all of the problems you have ever encountered in your lifetime. Have you learned a lesson from each and every one of them? Most people have. And yet the average person avoids problems like the plague rather than embracing them and realizing that every difficulty will pass and leave us with little nuggets of wisdom that we can use in other areas of our lives.

The real key to mastery of yourself is persistence. Nothing can stop the person who simply refuses to be stopped. There is a solution to every problem and if you want something bad enough, you will find a way to get it. There is no success story without the presence of persistence. Cultivate this quality, it will never let you down.

The Fifth Key to Mastery: Raise Your Standards & Keep Pushing

A famous international boxing champion was once asked the secret to his phenomenal physique and fitness level. "I daily exercise my body against great resistance." Pushing his muscles against tremendous weight built him up into the elite athlete that he was. The same physical principle applies to your mind and the mastery of your inner and outer world.

On a daily basis, you must exert your willpower to do those things which you do not like to do. Do that which you fear and the fear vanishes into thin air never to return. When that feeling of procrastination sets in just as you are about to sit down to that long overdue project, throw it off and tap your true strength of character to get the job done. Each time you overcome these weak tendencies that may have held you back in the past, you take a bold step in the direction of your dreams. Each time you push yourself, just like pushing your muscles when you exercise, you grow tougher and more forceful. Soon what was once hard becomes easy.

It is also essential to raise your standards on a regular basis, every master does. Everyone reaches a plateau in any activity. You know you are at this level when things become too easy and the challenge is gone. Things get boring (just like a life without difficulties and challenges). Fight against staying on the plateau. To expand, grow and prosper, your aim must be set high on the stars. Keep getting better every day. Never accept anything but the very best from yourself. This is your essential nature, tap into it.

The Sixth Key to Mastery: Even the Teachers Have Teachers

Always keep an open mind. No matter how disciplined and successful you become, remember that even the giants have teachers. There is no one on this planet that cannot learn more, improve more and live a better life.

As soon as you close your mind to new opportunities and ideas, you close off a part of your self-mastery path and your quest will be harder to carry out. Maintain a sense of humility and realize that you can learn something from everyone. Every person that you meet every day is a teacher of some sort. Listen to what they have to say and open yourself to the knowledge that exists for the taking.

The Seventh Key to Mastery: Have Fun & Enjoy the Journey of the Master

If you follow and apply the concepts you have learned so far from this book along with the 30 Day Program to a Perfect Life (in Part III), you are assured of reaching a state of self-mastery and lasting Bliss. But you have learned earlier that happiness is not a destination that is to be reached after a long trek through this world.   Rather, happiness is a manner of travelling through your life. One of the greatest truths is that every moment of every day is pure perfection, whether you realize it or not. There is no chaos in the world and everything happens for a reason. Today, realize the perfection and wonders of your life and do not waste a single minute in regret about things in the past.   The past has no relevance to your future and the achievements of which you are capable.

As you refine yourself, developing your mind power, your body and Perfect Health along with your character, enjoy the journey towards your goals. Have fun and be playful. Every master through the ages has known and applied this principle for the Miracle of Successful Living.

The Eighth Key to Mastery: Share Your Knowledge

When all the wisdom of the wisest thinkers and philosophers throughout history is distilled, the purpose of our existence becomes clarified.   The overriding objective of our lives stands high above all other pursuits and is simply stated: we are here to give to others. As you move through the 30 Day program, you will note incredible transformations in yourself. You will have unlimited power to do all that you want, you will have greater peace of mind, you will have more confidence, more energy and more passion for your dreams. You will note distinct improvements in your health, wealth and character. You will grow fundamentally different and start to live in a new, more magical reality.

But none of these tremendous benefits will be meaningful unless you share your knowledge and experiences with others in an effort to help them realize the amazing potential which may be sleeping within them. This is the last and most important step on the journey to mastery of your life. It is the recognition that all of us in this very special world are somehow connected. We are all on this journey together and one of the most noble of pursuits is to help all those around you reach the heights they too are capable of soaring to.

This is the book I have always wanted to write. The fact that you are reading this makes it clear that you are committed to reaching for the very best that you can be in all facets of your life- be it your professional, social, sporting or spiritual. You seek excellence and this book will inspire you to attain it. This book is a total guide to fulfilling the great potential that exists within all of us and a motivator to assist you in reaching to greater heights. We have the power to change and to constantly excel- this is part of what makes us human. Each one of us has the power to achieve great things- each one of us. The key is to learn the philosophies, strategies and techniques which will allow for a realization of our greatness.

But this book is more than the common self-growth guides that those committed to success regularly read. This book contains wisdom that will allow you to develop your leadership skills, enhance your relations with anyone you come into contact with, develop a deeper understanding of human nature and strengthen your personal character. It will allow you to view life from the highest level and constantly perform at your peak. Nutrition, personal grooming and proven confidence enhancement techniques are provided as are relaxation strategies and other mind conditioning methods that will enhance your focus, creativity, memory and overall well- being.

In Part I, you were exposed to the powerful techniques of self-suggestion, positive association and visualization used by the elite athlete to achieve goals and to eliminate weaknesses. You explored tools to improve your concentration, mental toughness , discipline and will-power as well as noting eastern philosophies on longevity and the habit of happiness. Part I of this book has given you the essential tools of life mastery and personal excellence. Part II now gives you the 200 Top Success Secrets to start MegaLiving!

1. Sleep less. This is one of the best investments you can make to make your life more productive and rewarding. Most people do not usually need more than 6 hours to maintain an excellent state of health. Try getting up 1 hour earlier for 21 days and it will develop into a powerful habit.

2. Set aside 1 hour every morning for personal development matters. Meditate, visualize your day, read inspirational texts to set the tone of your day, listen to motivational tapes or read some great literature. Take this quiet period to vitalize and energize your spirit for the productive day ahead.

3. Do not allow those things that matter the most in your life be at the mercy of activities that matter the least. Use your time effectively-it is your most valuable resource.

4. Use the rubber band method to condition your mind to focus solely on the most positive elements in your life. Place a rubber band around your wrist. Each time a negative, energy sapping thought enters your mind, snap the rubber band. Through the power of conditioning, your mind will associate pain with negative thinking and you will soon possess a strongly positive mindset.

5. Always answer the phone with enthusiasm in your voice and show your appreciation for the caller. Good phone manners are essential. To convey authority on the line, stand up. This will instill further confidence in your voice.

6. Throughout the day we all get inspirations and excellent ideas. Keep a set of cards (the size of business cards; these are available at most stationary stores) in your wallet along with a pencil (pens often leak) to jot down these insights. When you get home, put the ideas in a central place such as a coil notepad and review them from time to time.

7. Set aside every Sunday evening for yourself and be strongly disciplined with this habit. Use this period to plan your week, visualize your encounters

and what you want to achieve, to read new materials and inspirational books, to listen to soft soothing music or to simply relax.

8. Always remember the key principle that the quality of your life is the quality of your communication. This means the way you communicate with others and, more importantly, the way you communicate with yourself. What you focus on is what you get. If you look for the positive this is what you get. Its as simple as that.

9. Stay on purpose, not on outcome. In other words, do the task because it is what you love to do or because it will help someone or is a valuable exercise. Don't do it for the money or the recognition. Those will come naturally. This is the way of the world.

10. Laugh for five minutes in the mirror each morning. Steve Martin does. Laughter activates many beneficial chemicals within the body that place us into a very joyous state. Laughter also returns the body to a state of balance. Laughter therapy has been regularly been used to heal persons with varied ailments and is a wonderful tonic for life's ills.

11. Light a candle beside you when you are reading in the evening. It is most relaxing and creates a wonderful, soothing atmosphere.

12. To enhance your concentration and powers of focus, count your steps when you walk. This is a particularly strong technique. Take six steps while taking a long inhale, hold your breath for another six steps, and then exhale for six steps. If six steps is too long for the breaths, do whatever you feel comfortable with. You will feel very alert, refreshed and internally quiet and centered after this exercise.

13. Learn to meditate effectively. The mind is naturally a very noisy machine which wants to move from one subject to another like an unchained monkey. One must learn to restrain and discipline it if one is to achieve anything of substance and to be peaceful. Meditation for twenty minutes in the morning and twenty minutes in the evening will certainly provide you with exceptional results if regularly practiced for six months. Learned men of

the East have been advancing the many benefits of meditation for centuries.

14. Learn to be still. Develop the skill of sitting quietly, enjoying the powerful silence. Silence indeed is golden. As the Zen master once said, it is the space between the bars that holds the cage.

15. Enhance your will-power; it is likely one of the best training programs you can invest in. Here are some ideas to strengthen your will and become a stronger person:

a) Do not let your mind float like a piece of paper in the wind. Work hard to keep it focused at all times. When doing a task, think of nothing else. When walking to work, count the steps that it takes to get all the way to the office. This is not easy but your mind will soon understand that you hold its reins and not vice versa. Your mind must eventually become as still as a candle flame in a corner where there is no wind.

b) Your will is like a muscle. You must first exercise and then push it before it gets stronger. This necessarily involves short term pain but be assured that the improvements will come and will touch your character in a most positive way. When you are hungry, wait another hour before your meal. When you are labouring over a difficult task and your mind is prompting you to pick up the latest magazine for a break or to get up and go talk to a friend, curb the impulse. Soon you will be able to sit for hours in a precisely concentrated state. Sir Issac Newton, one of the greatest classical physicists the world has produced, once said:"if I have done the public any service, it is due to patient thought." Newton had a remarkable ability to sit quietly and think without interruption for very long periods of time. If he can develop this so can you.

c) You can also build your will power by restraint in your conduct with others. Speak less (use the 60/40 Rule=listen 60% of the time and speak a mere 40% if that). This will not only make you more popular but you will learn much wisdom as everyone we meet, every day has something to teach us. Also restrain the urge to gossip or to condemn someone who you feel has made a mistake. Stop complaining and develop a cheerful, vital and strong personality. You will greatly influence others.

d) When a negative thought comes to your mind, immediately replace it with a positive thought. Positive always dominates over the negative and your mind has to be conditioned to think only the best thoughts. Negative thinking is a conditioned process whereby the negative patterns are conditioned over and over. Rid yourself of any limitations and become a powerful thinker.

16. Make an effort to be humorous throughout the day. Not only is it beneficial from a physical viewpoint but it diffuses tension in difficult circumstances and creates an excellent atmosphere wherever you are. It was recently reported that members of the Tauripan tribe of South America have a ritual where they awake in the middle of the night to tell each other jokes. Even the tribesmen in the deepest of sleep wake to enjoy the laugh and then return to their state of slumber in seconds.

17. Become a highly disciplined time manager. There are roughly 168 hours in a week. This surely allows plenty of time for achievement of the many goals we desire to accomplish. Be ruthless with your time. Set aside a few minutes each morning to plan your day. Plan around your priorities and focus on not only those tasks which are urgent but not important (i.e., many telephone calls) but especially on those which are important but not urgent for these allow for the greatest personal and professional development. Important but not urgent activities are those which produce long-term, sustainable benefits and include exercise, strategic planning, the development of relationships, professional education. Never let the things which matter most be at the mercy of those that matter least.

18. Associate only with positive, focused people who you can learn from and who will not drain your valuable energy with complaining and uninspiring attitudes. By developing relationships with those committed to constant improvement and the pursuit of the best that life has to offer, you will have plenty of company on your path to the top of whatever mountain you seek to climb.

19. Stephen Hawking, one of the great modern physicists of the world, is reported to have said that we are on a minor planet of a very average star located within the outer limits of one of a hundred thousand million galaxies. Are your problems really significant in light of this? You walk this Earth for but a short time. Why not become devoted to having only a wonderful time. Sit down now and write out a list of all that you have in this world. Start first with your health or your family-the things we often take for granted. Put down the country we live in and the food we eat. Do not stop until you have written down fifty items. Once every few days, go through this list- you will be uplifted and recognize the richness of your existence.

20. You must have a mission statement in life. This is simply a set of guiding principles which clearly state where you are going and where you want to end up at the end of your life. A mission statement embodies your values. Over a period of one month, set a few hours aside to write down 5 or ten principles which will govern your life and which will keep you focused at all times. Examples might be to consistently serve others, to be a considerate citizen, to become highly wealthy or to serve as a powerful leader. Whatever the mission statement of your life, refine it and regularly review it. Then when something adverse happens or someone tries to pull you off course, you quickly and precisely return to your chosen path with the full knowledge that you are moving in the direction that you have selected.

21. No one can insult or hurt you without your permission. One of the golden keys to happiness and to great success is the way you interpret events which unfold before you. People who have attained greatness have an ability which they have developed to interpret negative or disempowering events as positive challenges which will assist them in growing and moving even farther up the ladder of success. There are no negative experiences only experiences which aid in your development and toughen your character so that you may soar to new heights.

22. Take a speed reading course. Reading is a powerful way to gain many years of experience from a few hours of study. For example, most biographies reflect the strategies and philosophies of great leaders or courageous individuals. Read them and model them. Speed reading will allow you to

digest large quantities of materials in relatively small periods of time.

23. Remember people's names and treat everyone well. This habit, along with enthusiasm, is one of the great success secrets. Everyone in this world wears an imaginary button that screams out "I WANT TO FEEL IMPORTANT AND APPRECIATED!".

24. Be soft as a flower when it comes to kindness but tough as thunder when it comes to principle. Be courteous and polite at all times but never ever be pushed around and ensure that you are always treated with respect.

25. Never ever discuss your health, wealth and other personal matters with anyone outside of your immediate family. Be very disciplined in this regard.

26. Be truthful, patient, persevering, modest and generous.

27. Soak in a warm bath at the end of a long , productive day. Reward yourself for even the smallest of achievement. Soon all your more important goals will be met and you will move to the next level of personal performance.

28. Learn the power of breathing and its relationship with your energy source. The mind is intimately connected with your breathing. For example, when the mind is agitated, your breathing becomes quick and shallow. When you are relaxed and focused, your breathing is deep and calm. By practising deep, abdominal breathing, you will develop a calm, serene demeanour that will remain cool in the hottest of circumstances.

29. Recognize and cultivate the power of autosuggestion. It works and is an essential tool in maintaining peak performance. We are all performers in one way or another and it is particularly valuable to use these techniques of athletes and public figures for our own enhancement. If you want to become more enthusiastic, repeat "I am more enthusiastic today and am improving this trait daily". Repeat it over and over. Purchase a legal notepad and write out this mantra 500 times. Do it for three weeks with regular practice and feel that this quality is developing. Very soon it will come. This is a strategy that

Indian wise men have employed for thousands of years to aid their spiritual and mental development. Do not be discouraged if the results are not immediate, they will certainly develop.

30. Maintain a diary to measure your progress and to express your thoughts. Writing out not only your successes but your troubles is one of the world's most effective methods of keeping people in optimum state and developing precision of thought.

31. Stress is simply a response which you create in the interpretation of an event. Two people might find that a given event results in quite different responses. For example, an after dinner speech might strike fear into the heart of an inexperienced speaker whilst a strong orator views it as a wonderful opportunity to share his thoughts. Understanding that the perceived negative effects of an event or task may be mentally manipulated and conditioned towards the positive will allow you to be a peak performer in all instances.

32. Read "The Seven Habits of Highly Effective People" by Stephen Covey. It contains a wealth of wisdom and powerful insights into further developing your character and enhancing your personal relationships.

33. Become a committed audio-tape user. Most self-mastery programs and books are now offered in this format. Listen to these inspirational materials on your way to work, whilst waiting in the line at a bank or while you wash the dishes in the evening. All down time can be very effectively used in this fashion. Use such opportunities to learn and continually expand your mind and its vast potential.

34. Try fasting one day every two weeks. During these fast days, drink only fruit juice and eat only fresh fruits. You will feel more energetic, cleansed and more alert. Fasting also has a salutary effect on your will-power as you are subverting the otherwise pressing impulses in your mind calling on you to eat more.

35. Keep a radio/cassette player at your office and listen to soft, soothing classical music throughout the day. By the magic of association, your work will also become something you enjoy even more and arouse a very pleasant feeling within you.

35. Budget your time on trips such that you can spend 1/2 hour in the airport bookstore. They always contain the latest and best self-mastery books and tapes given that those who travel by air are of a group that finds value in these materials.

36. Read "Awaken the Giant Within" by Anthony Robbins. This text will help you learn to run your brain more efficiently and effectively and inspire you to soar to new heights.

37. Remember that forgiveness is a virtue that few can develop but one that is most important to maintaining peace of mind. Mark Twain wrote that forgiveness is the fragrance the violet sheds on the heel that has crushed it. Practice forgiveness especially in those situations where it is seemingly difficult. By using your emotional forgiveness muscles more regularly, very soon petty wrongs, remarks and slights will not even touch you and nothing will penetrate your concentrated, serene mindset.

38. Empty your cup. A full cup cannot accept anything more. Similarly, a person who believes that he cannot learn any thing else will stagnate quickly and will not move to higher levels. A true sign of a secure, mature individual is someone who sees every opportunity as a chance to learn. Even the teachers have teachers.

39. The Two Minute Mind. An excellent exercise for developing concentration is to stare at the second hand on your wristwatch for two minutes and think about nothing else for that time. At first your mind will wander but after 21 days of practice, your attention will not waver during the routine. One of the greatest qualities a person can develop to ensure his success is the ability to concentrate/focus for extended periods of time.

40. Drink a cup of warm water before a speech. Ronald Reagan employed this strategy to ensure that he maintained his honey-smooth voice.

41. When you stand and meet someone, stand firm and steadfast. A telling sign of an unfocused, weak mind is constant fidgeting, shifting of the eyes and shallow breathing.

42. Act tough and you will be tough. Have courage and inspire others with your actions. But always be considerate.

43. Ask not what this world can do for you but, rather, what you can do for this world. Make service an important goal in your life. It is a most fulfilling investment of time.

44. Once a week, get up at dawn. This is a magical time of day. Go for a walk or simply listen to an old Ella Fitzgerald recording. Take a long, hot shower and do 100 pushups. You will feel alive and invigorated.

45. Remain slightly aloof. Do not let everyone know everything about you. Cultivate a mystique.

46. Master the art of public speaking. There are few natural speakers. One great trial lawyer stammered dreadfully but through courage and strength of conviction, he developed into a brilliant orator. Model anyone you think is a highly effective, influential communicator. Stand like him, smile like him, and talk like him. Visualize a picture of this person.

47. Seek out motivational speakers and lecturers committed to character training. Make it a point to attend such a lecture every few months to consistently renew the importance of personal growth in your mind. One top success coach has coined the term "CANI" for constant and never-ending improvement. This must be an illuminating principle for your life.

48. Read the wonderful book "Perfect Health" by Deepak Chopra. It will certainly open up new horizons for you in your quest for an optimal state of health.

49. To enhance your concentration, read a passage in a book you have never explored. Then try to recite it verbatim. Practice this for only 5 minutes a day and enjoy the results which follow after a few months of effort.

50. Try entering a 5 km running race and then a 10 km event. The adrenaline that flows from the experience of racing with several hundred other fitness-minded people is exhilarating.

51. Aromas have been proven to be an effective means of entering a state of relaxation. Purchase the essential oils of orange and clove bud from your local health food shop. Put a few drops of either oil within a cup of boiling water and inhale the sweet smelling steam for a few minutes. Then let the mixture sit in the room where you are resting. You will gain a sense of peace and serenity.

52. Cultivate the art of walking 1/2 an hour after you have finished eating your evening meal. Walks in natural settings are the very best.

53. Start a program of weight lifting at the gym. Strong people are mentally tough people.

54. Never argue with the person you work for- you will lose more than just the argument.

55. In terms of business attire, dark suits (navy blue and charcoal grey) reflect power, sophistication and authority. Have you ever seen a prime minister or president in a tan suit?

56. Regularly send handwritten notes to your business clients and to your other relations to strengthen the bond. Attach a recent article of interest to let the other person know that you value and respect the friendship.

57. Two of the fundamentals for a happy, joyful life are balance and moderation. One must maintain a balance of all activities and do nothing to extremes.

58. Drink Jasmine tea which can be obtained from any Chinese herbal shop. It is excellent for general health and is very relaxing.

59. Remember that effective time management makes you more rather than less flexible. It allows you to do the things that you really want to do rather than the things you really have to do.

60. Do not take personal development books as gospel. Read them and take whatever useful ideas you need. Some people feel they must do everything suggested and take the techniques to extremes. Every book has at least one tool or strategy of benefit. Take it and discard what you don't need.

61. Become an adventurer. Once every few months, plan to enjoy a new, thrilling activity such as white water rafting, scuba diving, windsurfing, rockclimbing, joining a martial arts club, sailing, deep sea fishing or camping. This will keep your life in perspective, bring you closer to those you share the activity with and keep you feeling invigorated and young.

62. Spend time with nature. Start camping or simply taking quiet walks in the forest. Carefully observe what surrounds you in the natural scene and keep your attention clearly on what is before you. Cultivate this habit.

63. Recall the wise saying "mens sana in corpore sano" which means in a sound body rests a sound mind. Never neglect the body which is intimately connected to the mind. Swimming, running and waking are excellent pursuits to do.

64. Be so strong that nothing interferes with your piece of mind. A well-known boxer was once unhappy. When asked why, he said that he had allowed himself to think a negative thought. Curb your desires and stay centered and focused-it gets easier with practice.

65. Do not eat 3 hours before sleep. This allows for smoother digestion and a more restful sleep.

66. Be careful about your reputation. If it is good it will take you to the highest of heights. But once tarnished, it will be difficult to retrieve. Always reflect on your course of action. Never do anything you would'nt be proud of telling your mother about. Have fun always but temper it with common sense and prudence.

67. Find mentors to model and who will guide you in your progress. The mistakes of the world have all been made once before-why should'nt you have the benefit of the experience of others? Find someone who has both courage and consideration for others, someone who is therefore mature. Your mentor must have only your best interests in mind and should be sufficiently senior to offer you good guidance on the subjects you seek assistance on. Everyone needs to feel appreciated and even the busiest of executives will find time to assist another who respects them and values their advice.

68. Make a list of all your weaknesses. A truly confident and enlightened person will note his weaknesses and seek to methodically improve them. Bear in mind that even the greatest and most powerful of persons have weaknesses. Some are better than others in hiding weakness. On the other hand, know your best qualities and cultivate, refine them.

69. Never ever complain. Be known as a positive, strong, energetic and enthusiastic person. Someone who complains, is cynical and always observing the negative in everything will scare people away and can never succeed at anything. From a purely psychological viewpoint, things are always created two times: once in the mind and once in actual reality. Focus on the positive, be so mentally tough that nothing takes you off your planned course to success. Visualize and firmly believe in what you want. It will most certainly come true.

70. Overlook the weaknesses of your friends. If you look for flaws you will most surely find them. Be mature enough to overlook the petty failings of others and see the good that each one inherently possesses. We can learn from everyone. Everyone has a story to tell, a joke to share and a lesson to learn. Open your mind to this and you will learn a tremendous amount.

Friends are so very important to a happy existence-especially those who you have shared many experiences and laughs with. Work hard to make your friendships, and all your relationships for that matter, stronger. Call your friends, buy them small gifts of books or other items you believe they might enjoy. The "law of the farm" applies here as to the rest of life- you will reap what you sow and relationships must be cultivated.

71. Be kind, considerate and courteous. But also be shrewd and know when to be tough and courageous. This is the mark of a well-defined character and you will surely command respect. It is most useful to read books on friendliness and enhancing relationships by being a good listener, showing others sincere appreciation and refining other inter-personal skills. But one, to truly succeed, must also recognize that worldly wisdom and shrewdness are essential skills to foster. Become an expert in human psychology and be able to read the essence of people. Never be taken advantage of and be aware of the politics around you. Stay above petty gossiping and office politics but appreciate that they indeed exist and know what is going on behind your back. Every great leader does.

72. Create your image as a highly competent, strong, disciplined, calm and decent individual. Find that crucial balance between working on the image that you project to the rest of the world and your inner character. Create a sense of mystery about yourself as the truly wise never show their hand. Do not tell everyone everything about yourself, your strategies and your aspirations. The successful citizens of this world think thrice before they speak because a word uttered can never be retrieved. Make things look easy and people will say you are naturally gifted. Speak only good things and people will flock to you. Never speak ill of others and all will know you will not malign them behind their backs. Build your character and live a highly principled life.

73. Familiarity breeds contempt is a very good rule. The stars remain far above the Earth. You must keep a distance from all but your closest of relations. Once people see everything of a leader he loses his aura and with it the authority and mystique he may have created. For example, Ronald Reagan is known to many as an excellent leader. He carefully cultivated his

image of a folksy, considerate politician who kept the interests of the United States first and foremost in his mind. At the gatherings of world leaders, he commanded attention and respect in his dark suits, surrounded by the trappings of power such as political aides, security officers and a convoy of limousines. As soon as he appeared, thoughts of authority and power came to our minds. Did you once see the President with his shirt off swimming at his pool? How about in his dressing gown after waking up after one of his long sleeps, hair tousled and beard grown? Reagan's handlers never allowed such glimpses because they detract from the perception of authority. The American nation was not exposed to these sights. In the Clinton Era things have changed and you see the President eating Big Macs and wearing baseball caps with a full business suit. Whilst these scenes may be endearing to the public, there is little doubt that President Clinton is more familiar to us, merely another one of us and, unlike the stars above us, much closer to the ground.

74. Learn to organize your time. It is incorrect to say that by becoming a meticulous time manager and living by a carefully defined schedule you become rigid and non-spontaneous. Rather, proper organization allows one to accomplish those goals which are truly important as well as enjoy leisure time. Good time management offers more time for fun and relaxation and not less. These important periods are scheduled into the week just like other commitments which may appear more pressing. Neither are sacrificed. Also, discipline yourself and stop wasting time on all those urgent but unimportant tasks (i.e., the ringing phones) and concentrate on the items and activities that are truly meaningful, those being activities that are important but not urgent such as professional readings, exercising and relaxation.

75. Keep well-informed as to current events, the latest books and popular trends. Read the newspaper daily. Not only will this allow you to converse with anyone and confirm your intellect but it will provide a constant and exciting stream of ideas for business ventures and other opportunities.

76. When choosing your life partner, remember that this is the most important decision of your lifetime. The marriage relationship offers 90% of all your support, happiness and fulfillment so choose it wisely. Consider

qualities such as affection, sense of humor, intelligence, beauty, maturity, temperament, compatibility and that indescribable characteristic of chemistry. If these are present, your relationship stands an excellent chance of great success. Move slowly and let no one press you into an uncomfortable decision.

77. Never ever discuss your personal development activities with anyone. They may not understand the value of this and, further, will take away your credit when you meet with success by saying that you relied on techniques etc. Keep this personal as these personal growth and renewal activities are for your knowledge and benefit.

78. Schedule relaxation time into your week and be ruthless in protecting it. You would not schedule another activity into the time planned for an important meeting so why would you do the same for that essential time we must have for ourselves to reflect, unwind and recharge our batteries. These are the renewal activities that allow us to maintain peak performance and they are exceptionally valuable periods.

79. 83% of our sensory input comes from our eyes. To truly concentrate on something , shut your eyes and you will remove much distraction.

80. Be the master of your will but the servant of your conscience.

81. Develop the wonderful habit of a daily swim. It will promote excellent health, keep you relaxed and concentrated, lean and trim. It is not stressful on the body, provides a great workout for the lungs and requires little time to do. Remember that in a fit body resides a fit mind.

82. The man who is doing good today is ensuring his happiness for tomorrow.

83. The key to successful time management is doing what you planned to do when you planned to do it. Keep your mind fully on the task at hand. Only then will you achieve all your goals and have time for the things that matter most. Although it is imperative to be flexible (a bow too tightly strung will

soon break), following your planned schedule requires no more than simple discipline.

84. An excellent visualization technique: if you are worrying about something, picture the words of your worry on a piece of paper. Now ignite a match to the paper and watch the worry dissipate into flames. Bruce Lee, the great martial arts master employed this one regularly.

85. Compartmentalize your worry. Set aside a certain amount of time to ponder over a problem and map out an effective plan of attack and your options. Once this is done, have the mental fortitude not to come back to the problem and go over it again and again. The human mind is a strange creature-things we want to forget keep coming back and those things we want to remember are not there when we want them. But the mind is similar to a muscle and the more you flex it the stronger it will become. Make it your servant. Feed it only the best nutrition and information. It will serve you well and perform magic if you believe in it.

86. Peak performers are physically relaxed and mentally engaged.

87. To be at your performance peak mentally, your body must physically be loose and relaxed. It is now beyond dispute that there is a mind-body connection and when the body is supple, free from tension, the mind is clear, calm and focused as well. This is why yoga is such a beneficial activity. It keeps the body relaxed so the mind can follow. Basic stretching for 15 minutes a day is also an excellent idea to release the tension that builds up as a result of our life in this highly complex and fast moving, but wonderful world.

88. Prepare a detailed financial plan for the next few years and follow it. Seek out financial advice if you need it. Being wise with your money is one of the very best investments to make. Financial security leads to personal freedom.

89. U.S. President Bill Clinton read more than 300 books during his short time at Oxford University. Seek out knowledge and information. We have truly entered the age of massive information and those who are proactive can very much use this to their advantage. The more you know, the less you will fear.

90. Get into the excellent habit of reading something positive and inspirational before you go to bed and as soon as you awake in the morning. You will soon note the benefits and these thoughts will be with you throughout the day.

91. Make it one of your goals to develop a dynamic, charismatic personality. Such a quality is something each one of us has the potential to develop but few do. President Kennedy was a sickly youth but rose above his physical problems to be the most charismatic and exciting political figure in the history of the United States. Start small. Take a Dale Carnegie course on public speaking. Go to the library where you will find books on the fine art of conversation and personal grooming. Learn three clean and witty jokes and get in the habit of socializing. You will have fun and build a lasting network of friends and associates.

92. On the subject of conversation, a Chinese proverb states as follows: a single conversation across the table with a wise man is worth a month's study of books. Seek out the wise and learn from them. They are just waiting for that small spark of interest to tell you all that you need to know.

93. Lao-Tzu prized 3 essential qualities for a person of greatness: "the first is gentleness; the second is frugality; the third is humility, which keeps me from putting myself before others. Be gentle and you can be bold; be frugal and you can be liberal; avoid putting yourself before others and you can become a leader among men."

94. "When you cannot make up your mind which of two evenly balanced courses of action you should take-choose the bolder" said W. J. Slim. There is no substitute for courage and though the chance of stubbing your toe increases the more you walk, it is always better than going nowhere by

standing still. Take chances, take smart risks and you will meet with success beyond your dreams.

95. Become your spouse's number one supporter, the one who is always there supporting her and fuelling her hopes and dreams. Develop together and march confidently through the world as an army of two.

96. Think of three people who can provide you with inspiration, motivation and support for your goals and aspirations and plan to meet with each one of them over the next few weeks. Listen to them and brainstorm with them. Map out a strategy and take their wise counsel.

97. Make every one of your days a true masterpiece. Remember the old saying: "it's not who you think you are that holds you back but what you think you're not."

98. Just as valuable energy is wasted by spending time on activities that are of no value, energy can be wasted on loose thinking. Imagine that your mind has an energy measure of 1000 watts at its disposal. Each time your mind wanders of the project at hand, to a nagging worry, to all the things to do by the end of the day, 100 watts is lost. Quite soon the entire energy supply is gone. This is the nature of the mind. Fail to discipline it and your energy levels will be depleted and your accomplishments will be minimal. Control it and you will see great things happening. You will feel more powerful and achieve difficult tasks with ease. The 19th century philosopher Henri Frederic Amiel summed it up nicely: "for purposes of action, nothing is more useful than narrowness of thought combined with energy of will."

99. It has been rightly said that "you sow an action, you reap a habit. You sow a habit, you reap a character. You sow a character, you reap a destiny." The essence of a person is his character-make yours unique, unblemished and strong. Do not say you will do anything unless you will indeed do it. Speak the truth and measure your words wisely. Be humble, straightforward and peaceful.

100.   Remember the overriding law of nature: positive overcomes the negative.

101.   A contented mind is a continual feast. Greed and material desires must be curbed to achieve lasting happiness and serenity. Be happy with what you have. Do you really need all of those material possessions? One can develop contentment just as one develops patience, courage and concentration-practice it daily and with sincere desire.

102.   Make a new friend or acquaintance every day. Keep an updated list of all contacts close at hand.

103.   If you conquer your mind, you conquer the world.   -Indian proverb.

104.   Place greater importance on staying happy than amassing material possessions. A zest for life is developed and carefully nurtured through thoughtful activities and pursuits.

105.   Contrary to popular opinion, stress is not a bad thing. It is useful to allow us to perform at our peak levels and can assist us through the flood of chemicals it causes to be released within our bodies. What is harmful is too much stress, or more particularly, a lack of relief from stress. The times of stress must be balanced nicely with times of pure relaxation and leisure for us to be healthy and at our best. Many of the great leaders of our time were exposed to crushing workloads and the burdens of high office. But they prospered by developing strategies to balance the challenging times with fun and calming times. President Kennedy would have regular naps in his White House office. Winston Churchill had the same practice and slept for one hour every afternoon to stay alert, focused and calm. Not only is it essential to be physically relaxed to maintain and foster optimal health but one must couple this trait with mental serenity. Too often people think that vigorous exercise, good nutrition and pleasant leisure activities will be the panacea for all ills. These pursuits must be combined with positive thinking and peace of the mind itself for true happiness and longevity.

106. Get in the habit of taking mental vacations throughout the day. Visit Bermuda for five minutes in the morning. Visualize a swim in the Mediterranean in the afternoon and skiing down the slopes of the Alps just before you head for the subway at the end of your busy and productive day. Try this for two months and schedule these rest periods into your agenda just as you do your essential meetings or tasks. The rewards will be significant.

107. A change is as good as a rest. Whether this change is as major as a change of employment or as minor as a leisure pursuit which occupies your entire attention for an hour three times a week, these changes in routine, and mindset are entirely beneficial. In selecting the activity, try to find something totally engaging which requires deep concentration so that your mind is free from the mundane but seemingly important aspect of your day. Many executives are becoming involved in the martial arts for just this reason. If your mind wanders for even a split second, a harsh lesson is soon learned. Pain is the great motivator and always will be.

108. Study these 10 fundamentals of happiness:
    *Pursue a productive, exciting and active life
    *Engage in meaningful activities every minute of every day
    *Develop an organized, planned lifestyle with little chaos
    *Set realistic goals yet keep your mark high
    *Think positively and do not afford yourself the luxury of a negative thought
    *Avoid needless worry and consideration of trifling matters
    *Devote time to fun
    *Develop a warm, outgoing personality with a sincere love of people
    *Get in the habit of giving more than receiving
    *Learn to live in the present. The past is water under the bridge of life.

109. Strive to be humble and live a simple life.

110. Read "A History of Knowledge" by Charles Van Doren which chronicles the history of the world's ideas. In this one book is an absolute wealth of knowledge. Get it, read it and enjoy it.

111. Read "The Art of the Leader" by William A. Cohen. It is both inspirational and practical.

112. Develop that elusive quality known as charisma. The following are ten qualities of a charismatic leader:

1. Be committed to what you are doing
2. Look like a winner and act like one
3. Have big dreams, a vision and reach for the sky
4. Steadily advance in the direction of your goals
5. Prepare and work hard at every task you do
6. Build a mystique around yourself
7. Be interested in others and show kindness
8. Have a strong sense of humour
9. Be known for the strength of your character
10. Have grace under pressure. John F. Kennedy said that "the elusive half-step between middle management and true leadership is grace under pressure."

113. In work, love and life, play hard and play fair.

114. Do not talk when you are listening. Interrupting is one of the most common discourtesies. Listen aggressively with the full scope of your attention. You will be amazed at what you will learn and how your counsel will soon be sought out by many.

115. "Anybody can become angry-that is easy; but to be angry with the right person, and to the right degree, and at the right time, and for the right purpose, and in the right way- that is not within everybody's power and is not easy." -Aristotle

116. Knowledge is power. People who have achieved great success are not necessarily more skillful or intelligent than others. What separates them is their burning desire and thirst for knowledge. The more one knows, the more one can achieve. Great leaders have techniques to allow them to arrive at the top of the mountain. Read the biographies of the world's leaders and

learn from their habits, inspirations and philosophies. Cultivate the important art of modelling.

117. All the answers to any questions are in print. How to improve as a public speaker, how to improve your relations with others, how to become fitter or develop a better memory- all aspects of personal development are dealt with in books. Therefore, in order to achieve your maximum potential, you must read daily. But, in this age of information, you must be ruthless in what you consume. Focus on your goals and read only those materials that will be an asset to you. Do not attempt to read everything for you are busy and have other tasks at hand. Choose what is important and filter out what is of no value. Begin with a solid newspaper every morning for an excellent summary of the key events of the day. Many high achievers read three or four papers each day- especially those involved within political pursuits. Also ensure that your readings are broadly based. For example, you may wish to read history, business, Eastern philosophy, health books etc. Then go to the library and develop the habit of making regular visits. Read the classics from Hemingway to Bram Stoker. Read history, with all its lessons on life and for the future and read biology for a new perspective on life. Look under the heading of success at the library and you will be amazed at what you will find. Inspirational stories of people who developed greatness in the face of adversity. Strategies for improving yourself physically, mentally and spiritually and texts to tap the vast and unlimited power for success and energy that certainly exists within us. Drink deeply from such books. Surround yourself with them and try and read them constantly whether on the subway each day or before you go to bed. Let them inspire and motivate you.

118. Get in the habit of breakfast meetings. An early meal to touch base with a friend or business associate is a most pleasant way to start the day and allows you to maintain your contacts in the face of a busy schedule.

119. If you live in a flat, always ensure that it is very bright and has a swimming pool. A pool is especially important because it will allow you to have exercise no matter how busy your schedule is due to the convenience. There is nothing like a refreshing swim after a long, productive day. You will

feel excellent and sleep like a baby.

120. "Excellence is an art won by training and habituation. We do not act rightly because we have virtue or excellence, but rather we have those because we have acted rightly. We are what we repeatedly do. Excellence, then, is not an act but a habit. "

-Aristotle

121. A single conversation across the table from a wise man is worth a month's study of books.   -Chinese proverb

122. If you have a choice of taking two paths, always take the more daring of the two. Calculated risk taking often produces extraordinary results.

123. Everyday, get away from the noise, the crowds and the rush and spend a few hours alone in peaceful introspection, deep reading or simple relaxation.

124. That which any person who has walked this Earth has achieved you can achieve with the right mental attitude, perseverance and industry. Limiting thoughts and mental images must be banished and one's focus must be on the attainment of goals that are truly important.

125. Get into the habit of memorizing beautiful poetry. Not only will it be a great source of entertainment but it will quickly lift your intellectual functions to a higher level by improving your memory, concentration and mental agility.

126. Keep your words soft and arguments hard.

127. Break the worry habit by putting things in perspective and laughing over the small setbacks. Repeat to yourself that "this will soon pass" (over and over). Then take a sheet of paper, write out every worry on your mind and allot a certain period of time to worry about the problem, isolate the precise problem and formulate a powerful line of attack. By this practical technique, your negative, energy sapping habit will be a faint memory of the past.

128. Be known as that person who goes the extra mile. The person who works longer than others. Who takes on the extra assignments and follows them through with great success. The person who always remembers others and who makes family members feel truly special. Be a standout. Be the person with a balance in life of excellence in professional, family and personal growth matters. Be a star that shines brightly for all others to admire.

129. Become a committed and sincere networker. Cultivate new friendships. You will truly be surprised where people end up over the years and how small, kind gestures will help you later on in life. Treat everyone who crosses your path as if they are the most important person in your world. You will certainly meet with great success.

130. When you look for something you will find it. If you constantly say to yourself and think that you will meet with exceptional success, you will surely meet it. You must keep those goals you desire to achieve at the forefront of your mind throughout the day. Repeat your ambitions at least five times a day and visualize yourself achieving them. If your goal is to be rich, picture the house you will be living in, the car you will be driving, what it will feel like to be rich and the pleasure of attaining your goals in life. Repeat your ambition over and over until you have complete certainty that you will attain your desires and eventually you will.

131. Develop a sense of wonder about the world. Be an explorer. Find pleasure in the things that others take for granted. Stop and actually listen to that wonderful street musician playing the saxophone. Read that classic book that your father loved so much. Plan to get away from the city next week and visit a secluded, powerfully natural place for a few days.

132. Send people cards on their birthdays and little notes from time to time showing them that you care about them and were thinking about them. We are all busy but if you spend only five minutes a week to send out a card to a friend or family member, by the year end you will have sent out 52 cards. This is a small investment for the dividends that are guaranteed to follow.

133. Remember and use people's names when you talk to them. A person's name is a uniquely sweet sound to them.

134. Go outdoors and look up into the blue sky for half an hour. Note the supremely strong feeling that you get when you are connected to nature. Get away from your rigid schedule today and spend the afternoon with nature. Walk to the woods and sit by a cool stream. Go fishing or rent a canoe. Getting away from your routine will provide a refreshing release and make you feel wonderful when you eventually do come back.

135. Once every few weeks, leave your watch at home. In this society, we often become bound to the clock and soon it governs our every action like a rigid taskmaster. Go through the day doing precisely what you wish to do and for however long you wish to do it. Spend time with that special person without having to run off to your next appointment. Savour the moments and focus on what is truly important rather than those mundane things that somehow take on a greater importance than they really deserve.

136. Laugh at work and be known as a positive achiever.

137. An idea gives rise to a mental image. A mental image will then generate a mental habit out of which a mental trait ultimately blossoms.

138. Recognize the tremendous power of opposition thinking. This simple technique simply involves the substitution of a positive thought each and every time a negative or limiting thought enters your mind and begins to detract from your focus. For example, on a Sunday evening, you may think "I wish I did not have to return to work tomorrow after such a pleasant and relaxing weekend." Immediately replace this defeating thought pattern before it begins to take hold by thinking the opposite. For example you might think "I cannot wait to return to the office given the exciting projects on the go and the wonderful sense of accomplishment I receive after a productive, challenging week." Then think how fortunate you are to have a job and one that you can grow in by your own efforts and productivity. Make a list of all of the positive attributes of your position and repeat them over and over. Soon the negative pattern will be broken and you will look toward the

wonderful week ahead with that most fabulous of qualities: ENTHUSIASM.

139. Get deep into the habit of personal introspection. Spend ten minutes every night before you go to bed in self-examination. Think about the good things you did during the day and the bad actions you may have taken which you must change in order to excel and grow. This valuable habit will soon allow the eradication of your negative qualities (ranging from procrastination to gossiping to insulting others) and will sharpen the mind as a muscle. After steady practice, a time will eventually come when the mistakes you make are few indeed and your personal power will move to the highest level.

140. The most efficient and effective alarm clock ever developed lies within our own minds. If you do not believe this, try the following:

1. *Sit in an easy chair or on the edge of your bed approximately ten minutes before you go to bed.*

2. *Shut your eyes and gently rest your hands on your knees.*

3. *Breathe deeply for a few minutes (inhale to the count of five, hold to the count of ten and exhale fully).*

4. *Repeat the following command to yourself at least twenty times: "I will awake at (the desired time) feeling fresh, alert and enthusiastic." This command must be said with feeling and emotion. Then take a few seconds to visualize yourself waking up at the desired time (the more detailed the mental picture the better) and imagine how great you will feel. You will soon wake up at the desired moment after little or no practice.*

141. Some men see things as they are and say "why?". I dream of things that never were and say "why not?"   - George Bernard Shaw

142. Use these strategies to improve the quality of your mind-calming meditation:

1. Practice meditation at the same time each day, and in the same place so that your mind becomes accustomed to entering the desired serene state as soon as you enter the peaceful place.

2. The early morning is undoubtedly the most powerful time to meditate. Indian yogis believe that the pre-dawn time has almost magical qualities which aid in achieving the super-peaceful state so many meditators attempt to attain.

3. Before you start, command your mind to be quiet by using affirmations such as "I will be focused and highly calm now."

4. If thoughts do enter, do not force them out but simply let them pass like clouds making way for the beautiful blue sky. Picture that your mind is like a still lake without even a ripple.

5. Sit for ten minutes first and then increase the time every few sittings. After a month or two, you will not be interrupted by any pressing thoughts and will surely feel a sense of peace that you have never felt before.

143. Forge and foster great friendships as such relationships are essential for maintaining a healthy and successful life. Find a few minutes every day to jot down some warm wishes to an old friend or to place a telephone call to someone you have not had a chance to speak to for a while. Show compassion and sincere consideration for all your friends and watch the results which follow. Develop long lasting friendships by, first of all being a good friend. Also, make it a priority to seek out new friends no matter how many you may be fortunate enough to have. This is one of life's greatest joys which many of us miss.

144. Purchase a cassette or CD of Miles Davis's *Kind Of Blue* . It is a uniquely soothing compilation that will refresh and sooth you after a challenging and productive day. Music such as this is good for the soul.

145. Drown your appetite by drinking more water. It revitalizes the system and purifies the body. Also, get into the habit of eating soups and more complex carbohydrates such as rice, potatoes and pasta which feed your hunger with far less calories than other less healthy foods. You truly are what you eat and must ensure that your diet is designed to maximize your energy and mental clarity.

146. Develop the essential habit of punctuality for it is most important for high success. Punctuality reflects discipline and a proper regard for others. Without it, even the most sophisticated person appears slightly offensive. Do not be early and certainly never be late. Budget your time and, should you arrive early, take a walk or simply relax for a few moments to ensure that you arrive on time as requested. You will be appreciated and welcomed always if you cultivate this important quality that appears so rarely these days.

147. The telephone is there for your convenience, not for the convenience of others who are attempting to contact you. If you are busy with a task, do not answer the phone or have someone answer the call so that you may return it at a more suitable time. Do not let such interruptions waste your time. Most phone calls are not important and last far too long anyway. There are so many important and fun things to do in life. The challenge is to respect precious time so that we can achieve greatness.

148. Wake up each morning and before you get out of bed, say a prayer or repeat your personal affirmation giving thanks for the day and all the positive things you will see and achieve this day. Make a conscious decision to make this the best day of your life and meet with pleasure, success and fun. If you believe it, it will most certainly happen.

149. Confide in your spouse/partner. This will strengthen the relationship and allow you both to grow at the same pace. It is also a wonderful tonic to share important or otherwise troubling things with the person you are most

close to.

150. Push yourself just a little bit harder and just a little bit farther each day. Do that thing that you have consistently put off. Write that thank you note or letter that you have forgotten for so long. Exercise your discipline muscles and they will rise to the occasion by imbuing your day with more drive and more energy.

151. All individuals who have attained the highest of levels generally have cultivated the essential mental habit of optimism. Without optimism, life loses its lustre and hardships appear at every step of the way. This is an essential life habit.

152. Today, write down the 7 best qualities of individuals who you admire and post this list on your bedpost. Then, each morning as you rise, focus on a new quality which you will strive to implement during the day. After one week, you will notice small differences in yourself. In one month, these traits will become firmly embedded. After two months, all those important qualities will be yours.

153. You have as many reputations as you do acquaintances as each person you know thinks differently of you. What should truly concern you is your character. You have full control of this and this is what you must develop, refine and cultivate. Once your character is strong and vigorous, then all else positive follows.

154. Consider yourself as an orange. Only what is really inside can come out. If you fill your mind with thoughts of serenity, positivity, strength, courage and compassion, when someone squeezes you, this is the only juice that can flow.

155. Our lives have been described as a parenthesis in eternity. We are but a small blip on the stage of the Universe. As we can take nothing with us when we finally leave, then the real meaning of our existence must be to give and serve others. Keep this in mind. When you wake up early in the morning, repeat the mantra: "I will serve others today, I will care for others

today and I will be kind today." This kind of living will bring you huge returns if you stay on the purpose of aiding others rather on the outcome of personal gain.

156. Be known as an innovator at your place of work. Sit down over the next week and write out ten suggestions for your supervisor as to how to improve the work being done and the quality of the workplace itself. Be known as an idea person willing to discover challenges and tackle them with zest and enthusiasm.

157. Learn to laugh at yourself.

158. Keep open the windows of your mind.

159. Try to go through one full day without saying "I". Focus on others. Listen to others and you will learn wonderful new things as well as gain friendships.

160. Spend one hour a day in full silence except in answer to direct questions. Even then, answer directly and without extending the conversation unduly. We, so very often, talk around subjects and repeat ourselves. This exercise will not only build your will power but develop clarity and precision of language which is essential for effective communication.

161. Each day, do two things that you do not like doing. This may be the preparation of a report you have been putting off or shining your shoes. It does not matter how small the task, just do it! Soon these chores will not seem so bad, your personal power will increase and your productivity will soar. Try it because this is an age old technique for building strength of character.

162. True happiness comes from only one thing: achievement of goals whether they be personal, professional or otherwise. Time spent on activities which offer little reward aside from a fleeting feeling of relaxation (television watching is the best example), is time lost forever. Relaxation is essential but choose the most effective means and spend your time in productive pursuits

that will slowly move you along the path of accomplishment. Happiness comes from doing not sleeping.

163. Napoleon III of France had a special ability to remember the names of all those he met. His secret was to say "so sorry, I missed your name" after being introduced to a new person to have the name repeated and reinforced within his memory. If the name was difficult, he would ask for the proper spelling.

164. Develop an indomitable spirit along with courtesy and integrity. The repetition of these three traits will make you an exceptionally powerful individual respected by all. Exert your effort and personal influence to attain these qualities.

165. A valuable technique for defeating negative and self-limiting thoughts that can hamper you from attaining peak performance is the mental interrupt device. When a negative thought enters your consciousness, first you must become aware of it and have a strong desire to remove it for good. To do this, interrupt the negative train of thought by doing something to break and banish the self-limiting pattern. When the bad thought enters, you may pinch yourself and say "I am strong and weak thoughts are gone", or you may shout out loud or do anything that will divert your attention and remove the negative focus. By practising this technique, you will see a marked decrease in the negative thoughts that most normal people have, paving the way to the mindset of a true winner.

166. Taking time from your busy work and family schedule to focus on personal growth activities is essential and is never to be considered a waste. Taking one hour from your hectic morning to go for a run or brisk walk might seem impossible to some but you will make the remaining hours much more productive and effective. This is something that has been proved time and time again and yet we consistently get caught up in the apparent immediacy of our routine and fail to see the forest for the trees.

167. Read more, learn more, laugh more and love more.

168. Pick five relationships that you desire to improve over the next six months. Write out the names of these people and under each name detail why you want to improve the relationship, how you plan to do so and in what time frame. This is simply another facet of goal setting- the action which will always yield excellent results in any of life's fields. Become committed to becoming a better husband, father, friend and citizen. Be creative in your actions aimed at showing your affection for others and appreciation for their kindness. Sending notes is fine but consider unique and thoughtful measures ranging from a romantic picnic in the country with your partner to an early morning fishing trip with an old friend.

169. Remember the power of prayer.

170. An excellent investment in your personal growth is the six tape series of Reverend Norman Vincent Peale entitled "The Power of Positive Thinking". Get it and listen to it over and over. It is packed full of strategies and techniques that, without fail, will ensure that you will live a long, happy productive and prosperous life.

171. Consider purchasing a pocket organizer which may prove to be an excellent tool for scheduling, keeping track of your commitments and keeping the responsibilities of your life in fine order. One can be purchased at a reasonable price.

172. Browse second-hand bookstores every few months searching for lost treasures of character building books. You will find gems on public speaking, improving your habits, time management, personal health and other important subjects for low prices. Some of these older texts are the very best and come from an age where every young person was under an obligation to develop discipline and good life habits regularly.

173. Read *The Magic of Believing* by Claude M. Bristol. It will allow you to release the powerful forces which most certainly exist in your mind but may presently be untapped.

174. Be known as someone with a cool head, warm heart and great character. Your presence on this earth will long be remembered.

175. It has been said that doing something for others is the highest form of religion. Every week, out of the 168 hours available, spend a few in service to others. Many say that such selfless service soon becomes a key focus within their lives. Give your time at a seniors home or to needy children. Teach someone how to read or offer to give a public lecture on a subject on which you are an expert. Simply take action and do something.

176. Fill your home with bright, fresh flowers. This is one of the best investments you can make.

177. Get to know and enjoy your neighbors. They make life pleasant and can provide helpful resources when you least expect it.

178. Recognize the power of mantras and the repetition of positive, powerful words. Indian sages have employed this technique for thousands of years to live a positive, productive and focused life. Create your own personal mantra which you can repeat daily to enhance and strengthen your character and spirit.

179. When the breath is still and strong, so is the mind.

180. Use the following visualization from time to time. Sit down in a quiet place and picture that you will only be on the earth for another day. Who would you call, what would you say and what would you do. These questions will give you some important insights into what outstanding actions you must endeavor to complete.

181. Study the following evidence of high character:
    1. Precision & clarity of thought and speech
    2. Refined and gentle manners
    3. The power and habit of introspection
    4. The power of personal growth
    5. The power to achieve your goals & dreams

182. "Youth is not a time of life; it is a state of mind. People grow old only by deserting their ideals and by outgrowing the consciousness of youth. Years wrinkle the skin, but to give up enthusiasm wrinkles the soul... You are as old as your doubt, your fear, your despair. The way to keep young is to keep your faith young. Keep your self-confidence young. Keep your hope young."
- Dr. L.F. Phelan

183. Explore the healing powers of Chinese herbal medicine and similar Eastern strategies for maintaining a state of perfect health (consult an expert at all times or take a formal course on the subject to gain powerful insights into this most useful area of healing).

184. Be certain to organize your time around the true priorities of your life. As Stephen Covey has noted: "it is easy to say no when there is a deeper yes burning within."

185. Slow down your pace of life. In this complex age, we are running our lives at a frantic pace. Focus on what is truly important and start undertaking activities that will slow you down and rekindle the natural, calm pace within us. Sit in the grass and watch the blue sky for half an hour-at first, it is not as easy as one would think and the urge is to get up after only a few minutes of such useful relaxation. Once you get used to a healthier pace with time outs for the pleasures of life, the other activities will become more efficient and enjoyable.

186. Try eating only fruit and milk for a full day. You will notice a surge in your energy level and a lightness in your walk. Big meals require a significant amount of energy that could be directed toward other more productive pursuits.

187. Value your spouse's laugh and keep your partner's picture close by your work desk for inspiration and pleasant thoughts throughout the day.

188. If you are married, have your partner's initials and your own engraved on the inside of your wedding bands along with the date of your marriage. This is useful not only in case the rings are lost but to provide you both with personalized keepsakes that may be passed down to successive generations.

189. What you put in is what comes out. Avoid violent movies, trashy novels and other negative materials. Have a disciplined, tranquil and peaceful mind.

190. Do 100 sit ups a day and do not break this habit. Strong abdominal muscles are very helpful to ensuring that you enjoy peak health and injury free days. They also maintain your appearance and confidence level.

191. Be the most honest person that you know.

192. Curb your worldly desires and you will strengthen your will. He who is deeply bound to material things runs into difficulty and unhappiness when they are taken away. Most people enjoy worldly objects but do not become bound or wedded to them. Live a simple, uncluttered and productive existence.

193. If you have not laughed today, you have not lived today. Laugh hard and loud.

194. Read *The Charisma Factor- How to Develop Your Natural Leadership Ability* by Robert J. Richardson and S. Katharine Thayer. It is a superb book for any aspiring leader or a current one who seeks to advance to the next level.

195. Travel often. The perspective offered by visiting new lands is important and allows one to appreciate the existence that we generally take for granted.

196. Each month set a physical fitness goal for yourself. Start to swim in July or learn to ski in January. The key is to arrive at a goal for the month, write it down, consider how to execute it and then, as the NIKE ad says: "Just Do It!".

197. Things are always created twice. There is always the mental creation which precedes the physical creation. Just as plans for a house must first be drafted on paper before the house is started, so too should your day be planned and organized within your mind early in the morning before the day begins. Visualize the wonders you desire this life to bring and they will materialize as your subconscious mind starts to focus on this attainment of goals. This is a true law of nature.

198. Walk to work and notice the wonderful beauty in nature.

199. Sleep less, spend less, do more, live longer and be greater.

200. Read this book over and over & share it with others!

The Ultimate Action Plan For Mastery of Your Mind, Body & Character

Welcome to the MegaLiving! program. A truly revolutionary personal growth plan that is holistic in its approach. It will unleash the incredible potential in all three of the key aspects of your life: your mind, your body and your character.

This program is designed to provide you with **all** the essential strategies needed to transform you into a peak performer at the game of life. No matter how finely tuned your mental attitude, body and character currently is, this 30 day program has all the ingredients to take your life to its highest level. If you use your personal power to devote at least an hour a day to the program, applying and learning the concepts consistently, you will certainly change your life.

Each day, you will meet with little victories and will start to gain a magical momentum and love for self-growth that will be unstoppable. The exercises given *must* be done in order to get any benefit from the program. And if you will give it a chance, your 30 hour commitment over this month will lead you to the energy, health, serenity, attitude and motivation that you have been searching for. Follow this incredible program to achieve all your dreams. Follow this program, put your heart into it and you will see that life you have longed for-your Perfect Life.

The program is especially simple and easy to follow. Each of the following 30 pages refers to a single day of the program. Each day will have exercises, success tips or philosophies which you must apply that day. Use the Success Log at the end of the book to chart your daily progress. It is important that you enter your results into the Success Log every day to provide you with a measure of your discipline and to give you the momentum and inspiration to continue. Now start the program that will change your life: MegaLiving!

DAY 1

Date:_____

Part I: THE MIND   *Goal Setting Workshop*

Today is the first day of the rest of your life. You must start preparing for what you want to be in twenty or thirty years this very day, not twenty or thirty years from today. You have learned in Part I & II of the mind's true potential and that you have the incredible power to transform your life in a second if you really want to. Today, make those changes you have put off for so long. Start living your dreams & finally create a new personal destiny.

List your top ten mind improvement goals for the next 30 days

      i) _____
      ii) _____
      iii) _____
      iv) _____
      v) _____
      vi) _____
      vii) _____
      viii) _____
      ix) _____
      x) _____

Go over this list at least three times today, repeating your burning commitment to achieving these goals & a clear date by which you will have attained them. Let the power of autosuggestion work for you as it has worked for so many success stories of the past. Now think of all the pain you will feel if you do not make these improvements-really see & feel it. Finally, think of all the pleasure you will have if you indeed accomplish the above goals, how increased concentration, mental focus & supreme confidence will enhance your life. Please review your mental goal list every remaining day of the MegaLiving! program, even if for only a few seconds.

Part II: THE BODY

Today is the first day of your new physical reality. Over the next 29 days, you will learn secrets for taking your body and physiology to its highest level. You will learn how to condition it for peak health and peak life performance. Welcome to the path of physical mastery.

List your top 5 physical goals

      i) _____
      ii) _____
      iii) _____
      iv) _____
      v) _____

Part III: THE CHARACTER

List the top 5 improvements in your character (your public & private self) which you are determined to have over the coming month. Consider their importance and repeat them aloud when you awake & immediately before you sleep for the next 29 days.

Day 2

Date:_____

Part I: THE MIND   *The Power of Concentration*

Without the ability to concentrate for long periods of time and to focus your thoughts on a single purpose or goal, there can be no real progress and no lasting life achievement. Concentration also brings with it a quiet serene mind, one that does not succumb to every weak thought passing by. A serene mind brings with it a healthier body as your health is clearly rooted in your thoughts.

Practice the following 2 concentration exercises every remaining day of the program for at least a total of 15 minutes:

Exercise 1:   **The Burning Candle**

Find a very quiet spot at a very quiet time. Light a candle in front of you, making sure the room is otherwise dark. Look at the candle for as long as you can & try not to blink. Study the shape of the flame, its texture and its movements. Do not take your mental focus away from the flame-if its drifts off to something else, gently pull your mind back and deeply concentrate on this beautifully empowering light. Each day you do this, your concentration will improve and you can focus without distraction for a longer time. You will also start to feel calmer and little things will no longer ruffle you.

Exercise 2:   **The Stepping Strategy**

One of the most effective methods used to improve those with weak thinking tendencies and a lack of concentration is step counting. The process is simple yet the results will be striking. As you are walking, inhale to six steps, hold your breath for another six and exhale for six more steps. Repeat the cycle and do not let your mind wander away from your step counting.

Part II: THE BODY   *The Power of Exercise*

Start your exercise program today and focus on cardiovascular conditioning. If you are not fit, a 15 minute walk in the fresh air at a moderate pace will be fine. If you are fit, do whatever sport you have been doing, whether swimming, running, squash or rollerblading, for an extra 15 minutes. The key is to push your body. Do some exercise every day for the next 30 if you want results.

Part III: THE CHARACTER   *The Power of Kindness*

Your character will be shaped slowly and steadily over time. By making little daily improvements, it will take on a new form and become full of strength, power and vitality. Today, reflect on one of your top character improvement goals noted yesterday. Develop a clear plan of why this new quality is important and what you will do to have it. One of the most valuable qualities is that of kindness to others. Kindness and consideration for those around you will ultimately give you lasting happiness as well as personal, professional and social respect. Start off your day by affirming aloud your commitment to becoming a kinder more considerate person. Then visualize your wonderful day unfolding in your mind's eye, taking care to focus on every possible opportunity to show kindness to others. See this happening and it will indeed happen.

Day 3

Part I: THE MIND   *The Power of Mental Conditioning & the 5 Questions of Success*

Today, you will learn the power of conditioning your mind for success. The key to achieving excellence in all areas of your life is to recognize that what you focus on you will have. If you focus on all that is good in your life and use mental pictures to fill your mind with beautiful images, the laws of Nature will act to make them into reality.

One of the best ways to direct your mind's focus is to use questions. From today onwards, start your day off with a winner's mindset by developing 5 Questions of Success. Some of the best are as follows:

      i)   How can I make today a living masterpiece & what action must I take?
      ii)   What do I have to be grateful for? (make a complete mental list)
      iii)   What can I do today to improve my mind, body and spirit?
      iv)   How can I contribute to the world in some small way?
      v)   What can I do to laugh & have fun today?

These questions should become part of your life. Just as you brush your teeth after you wake up, you must develop the habit of asking yourself these questions every morning. It will only take a few minutes and you can do it while you are in the shower. But they will very quickly change the way you feel and the way you act throughout the day. This simple formula will bring you lasting results and enrich your life.

Part II: THE BODY   *Getting back to Nature*

Nature has a brilliant effect on an overworked body and mind. Realizing the benefits of time with Nature is a first step to true relaxation and serenity. Today, make a plan for some event to get you in touch with the natural world around you . It may be as significant as a week camping and hiking in a national park or as simple as a walk in the woods behind your house for half an hour. The key is to focus all your attention on the surroundings and affirm the beauty and simplicity of the world. We make things much more complex than they are and taking this time for yourself to look up at that magnificent blue sky or sit alongside a still lake is something that you deserve. Try to make such activities part of your weekly exercise regimen.

Part III: THE CHARACTER   *Your Personal Success Journal*

You have decided to make your life a living masterpiece. It is now important to record your daily results, ideas, inspirations and challenges. There is something magical about writing things down. Your thoughts and focus becomes clearer and plans become burning desires when put into the written form.

You do not require anything expensive-a simple coil notebook will do nicely to start you off. Write daily if possible but do not worry if you miss a day or two. The main idea is to note down all your thoughts and how you plan to tackle any difficult situations. Journal writing has also become one of the most favored techniques to stop worrying. By writing any problems down, they stop running over and over through your mind. Once the problem is isolated, you can develop a precise plan of attack and your serene mindset will remain intact.

Day 4

Date:_____

Part I: THE MIND   *Autosuggestion & Dream-Building*

Autosuggestion must become one of your main tools for personal mastery. Through this age-old technique, a person without confidence will soon develop it, a person with no motivation may soon attain it and one without material wealth can ultimately have it.

Autosuggestion is simple and nothing more than an application of the following two-step formula:

      i)   Write down the goal you are determined to achieve (this can be anything from confidence to making a million dollars). Make certain that the goal is precise and clear.

     ii)   Read the desired goal aloud as many times as possible during the day but, at least before you get up and prior to sleeping. Do the repetitions (or mantras as they are often called) 10 times at a time and really believe that they will come true. A clearly defined goal, repeated regularly until it becomes a burning desire will come true when it is combined with that all-important ingredient of belief in its realization. Do not worry that it does not seem that it will come true under your present circumstances. Simply persist and follow this formula. Your mind will create the opportunities & the results.

Part II: THE BODY   *The Self-Massage*

A full-body massage will make you feel like a million dollars and can be done by yourself in just five minutes. The massage will lubricate your skin keeping it soft and supple, ease any tension in your muscles and correspondingly, calm your mind providing a deep sense of relaxation and peace.

Buy yourself a bottle of sesame oil (available form any health store). Heat up four or five tablespoons in the microwave, being very careful not to make it too hot as you will burn yourself. Then, in your bathroom, dip your fingers into the oil and start your body massage. Start with your feet and legs rubbing vigourously, massaging any tightness out. Then move to your stomach and abdomen where you should be more gentle and use clockwise circular motions. Next is the back, neck and arms. Finally, work your way on to your face, massaging your skin deeply. When the massage is complete, soak in a hot bath if possible. This caps off the relaxation strategy with a soothing activity and also removes the excess oil form your body. You can do the personal massage daily for best results or once a week when you wish to relax and have some time for yourself.

Part III: THE CHARACTER   *Enhancing Your Social Environment*

Today's exercise is simple. Go to your local bookstore or library and get a copy of Dale Carnegie's *How to Win Friends and Influence People*. Read it completely over the next week. Think deeply about its wisdom and start to apply its philosophy.

Day 5

Part I: THE MIND   *Mastery of Your Concentration Skills*

The key to success in life, you might be surprised to learn is simply mental concentration. With a concentrated mind, you will live not in the past, not in the future but in the present. When you learn to concentrate effectively, big problems become small and you can see things in the world that were previously invisible. You will be able to work more efficiently without the burden of a wandering mind that worries about past difficulties and actions. Things will come easy to you and you can move quickly to achieve your ambitions and desires. With concentration comes deep peace of mind.

The stronger your mind, the lovelier life becomes. Life is very much like a rose. There are thorns along the path but once you rise above them, there is true and lasting beauty. Remember the rose and its wonderful properties. Your exercise today is a fun one:

> *   Buy a single rose. Place it in a quiet spot and stare at it for as long as possible. Focus on its brilliant qualities, its splendid texture and fragrance. Do not take your sight or mind off the rose. Other thoughts will come into your mind if you have not trained it for concentration. Do not worry, gently let the thoughts pass away like a cloud moves through the blue sky and return your attention to the rose. Practice this essential exercise every day. It is among the most important. Once you can focus without interruption for twenty minutes, you will have reached the level where your mind is conditioned to do very special things for you. You will be amazed at the changes in life such mental toughness brings.

Part II: THE BODY   *Voice Conditioning: An Ancient Technique for Vitality*

The ancient Tibetans believed that the health of the body was controlled through the operation of seven spinning vortexes. When the vortexes slowed down, hormonal changes would cause the process of aging to set in. One of the vortexes, located deep in the neck, governs the vocal chords. If the voice is strengthened, the vortex is stimulated to produce an optimal state of health. This is why Tibetan monks would perform chants daily. Not only would such vocal conditioning enhance their all-important concentration skills but it would yield remarkable physical results in the form of peak health.

Exercise: Repeat "Mimm" over and over for at least 5 minutes a day. Perhaps the best time to do this is whilst you shower. For the best results, gradually lower your voice with each repetition until you can do the entire exercise in the lowest voice you have.

Part III: THE CHARACTER   *Courtesy*

"Manners maketh man" wrote a literary scholar many years ago. Showing politeness to everyone you meet will make your character mighty and dramatically improve your relationships. Today, make an action list of all the chances you will have to show courtesy to those around you, to show that you appreciate them. Then, use these opportunities to grow. Remember that no one can insult you without your permission. If any one is rude, do not stoop to their level but remain graceful and poised. Never raise your voice and be known as a highly self-disciplined person who is kind yet strong.

Day 6

Date:_____

Part I: THE MIND   *Becoming a Mental Explorer*

Mental stimulation is essential for good health and intellectual growth. Through this book, you have learned that you are likely only using 20% of your mind's potential. You must work hard and become the mental giant you are capable of being. Do not pay any attention to what others may have said about your abilities. Accept no limitations on yourself and what you can achieve because there are truly none.

You must become a mental explorer, an individual dedicated to learning about the powers of the mind and its incredible abilities. The first step is to have an open mind. Meditation, yoga, focusing and visualization are now a key part of the peak performance regimens of many of the world's top athletes. Seinfeld practices yoga daily and a significant number of business executives have found peace and good health through various meditation techniques.

Exercise: Go to your local library or bookstore and study some of the success literature, Pick up two of the stranger sounding titles and read them. Remain open to any new ideas you are exposed to in the field of personal development and try new things.

Part II: THE BODY   *Sleep Less & Live More*

Your body needs only about 6 hours of sleep per night to be in peak condition yet many people sleep 9 or 10 hours a night. There are only 168 hours in a week and so many fun, exciting things to do. One of the very best strategies to increase your productivity is to sleep one hour less per night. Sleeping too much is caused by a bad habit. To have a fuller, more accomplished life, break this habit and sleep only as much as you need.

Start off slowly and get up half an hour earlier tomorrow. After three days, cut back to the full one hour. You will notice that it gets much easier as time goes on. After three weeks, you will wonder why you wasted this time. A key principle to remember is that if you do anything for 21 consecutive days, it becomes a habit and much easier to do. Stick it out for this period and you will find that you suddenly have all the time you once said you never had. This is a powerful success secret which can positively impact on your life in a dramatic way.

Part III: THE CHARACTER   *The Abundance Mentality*

One of the primary laws of Nature is that the more you give and the more you serve others, the more you get. Too many people live with a scarcity mentality believing that if they share ideas, wealth or resources, there will be less left for them. This is the surest way to a life of little. Develop the habit of doing things for others, especially those in need. Give money to your favorite charity and do not shy away from public service. Work with others in both your business and the community. Shed the "us versus them" mentality and recognize the powers of synergy: two hands are stronger than one.

Day 7

Part I: THE MIND   *Your Photographic Memory*

One of the best kept secrets is that every person has a photographic memory locked deep inside of them-the key is to unlock it and bring it to life. When you last forgot something recall how it later came back to you. The fact was in your memory-it was just asleep and it needed to be prompted. All the details you have ever experienced are deep inside of your mind, waiting for the correct trigger.

The best way to tap your true memory potential is to give direct commands to your subconscious mind once it is in a state of readiness. To do this, you must first become very relaxed. Lie down on your back in a quiet place. Take twenty deep breaths, visualizing any tension leaving your body with each exhale.

Then, moving from your feet to the head, command the body to relax very deeply. For example, starting at your feet, say "my feet are now very heavy, I feel the heaviness." Then move up through the ankles, calves, thighs etc. Soon you will notice that your body is feeling very warm and entirely relaxed. At this stage, the subconscious part of your mind, which is exceptionally powerful, is most open to your commands. Repeat for five minutes, the following command:"I have a perfect memory, I can remember anything I want to recall at will, my memory is perfect and there to serve me."

Do this for a period of 21 days and you will notice a truly remarkable transformation.

Part II: THE BODY   *The Power of Breath*

Deep breathing will provide you with tremendous relaxation, vitality and energy. Deep breathing triggers the lymph, your body's sewage system which will give your cells more efficiency. Deep breathing also ensures that the blood is fully oxygenated, also providing for peak health.

Exercise: Deep breathing must occur to the following ratio: 1-4-2.
So if you inhale for 2 seconds, you should hold your breath for 8 seconds and then exhale to the count of 4. By practicing this cycle in repetitions of 10, 3 times a day, you will significantly increase your stamina and general state of health.

Part III: THE CHARACTER   *Persistence Breeds Success*

Every great person has failed on more than one occasion. Edison is said to have failed 10, 000 times before he finally struck it big with the lightbulb. When asked his secret to success, he replied: " I failed so many times that the only thing left to do was to succeed-I exhausted all the failures." As reported in the recent biography on Ted Turner, *It Ain't As Easy As It Looks*, what struck Turner's schoolmates was his extraordinary persistence. He always stayed with a goal until he eventually achieved it. Nothing can keep a good person down & the sooner you realize this the better. Rather than whining over problems and asking why they always seem to happen to you, start calling problems "challenges" and looking forward to them as tests of character and opportunities to learn and grow. You will always meet with challenges on the path of life but the champion learns to love them, learns from them and thrives on them.

Day 8

Date:_____

Part I: THE MIND   *More Concentration Conditioning*

The importance of mental concentration has been emphasized over and over in the MegaLiving! program. Today, you will learn yet another exercise to toughen up your mind, getting it ready for super performance.

Exercise: **The Two Minute Mind**

> This is a delightful exercise to strengthen a mind that suffers from wandering thoughts and a lack of the ability to concentrate. All you have to do is to stare at the second hand on your watch for 2 minutes. Give your full attention to the second hand and do not let any other thoughts occupy your attention. Your whole   world is in the movements of the second hand and use your will power to do this exercise properly. If you perform the technique 3 times a day, after 21 days, you will have developed a highly powerful mind and will notice a real difference in your energy level as well as in your overall mental agility.

Part II: THE BODY   *The Amazing Benefits of Yoga*

If there is one thing you can do to take your physical dimension to the highest plane it is to practise yoga. Classes are offered in all cities and the positions are easy to learn and wonderfully relaxing. Regular yoga practice will keep you serene, energetic, improve your complexion and digestion and enhance your overall muscle tone. Take this powerful step now! You have absolutely nothing to lose and so very much to gain.

Part III: THE CHARACTER   *The Value of Friendship*

Good friendships have been proven not only to make life more enjoyable but to give a longer one. Researchers from the University of Michigan found that those Tecumseh, Michigan residents who had the most family and friends lived the longest. Several studies have also found that married people live longer than their single counterparts.

Take today as an opportunity to dramatically improve your friendships. Pick five friends who you want to become closer with and write out their names. Then write out why you value their friendship. Finally, make a precise action plan to improve the friendship. It may be as simple as writing them a letter expressing your appreciation for their friendship & attaching an inspirational article of interest to them. You may buy your friend a book and drop it off personally to them saying: "I was at the bookstore and found this treasure I thought you would love." Take a friend out for a Sunday brunch or for a walk along the ocean to see the sun rise one morning. Even the act of writing out a "love letter" to a friend, which you never have to send, will improve the relationship because it clarifies in your mind the importance of this person in your life.

Day 9

Date:___________

Part I: THE MIND *Opting for Optimism*

Optimism will change your life. If you expect your life to be a living masterpiece you will be happier, live longer & have all that this magical world has to offer. Researchers have studied 99 young Harvard men for the effects of optimism. By the time the study was published in 1988, the cheerier individuals were less affected with severe illnesses than their pessimistic counterparts.

Optimism can be learned. Every day, think deeply about all the good things you have in life. Everyone has something to be grateful for. The difference between optimists & pessimists is that the former look for and find the good in everything. A pessimist always sees and remembers the bad. For example, an optimist looks back on the day & smiles at the kindness he received, the good meals he ate, the family he is fortunate enough to have been surrounded by and the good health that he has enjoyed. A pessimist sees none of this and focuses on one or two challenges that may have appeared. He then concludes that this "was a bad day" and continues to brood over these minor difficulties for the rest of the day. In the wonderful little book, *As a Man Thinketh,* James Allen wrote:

> Let a man radically alter his thoughts, and he will be astonished at the rapid transformation it will effect in the material conditions of his life.

Good thoughts are guaranteed to lead to sunny circumstances. Optimism is an essential condition for success. Resolve to curb your wandering mind now and start the habit of positive thinking today! Make certain every word you say is a good one, every thought you think is an inspiring one and every act you take an uplifting one. You have the power to MegaLive!

Part II: THE BODY *Strong Body=Strong Mind*

Rousseau said: "a feeble body enfeebles the mind." Physically strong people are mentally tough people. Build your physical strength and you will reap just rewards. Here are just a few of the exercises you should work into your exercise regimen today and every day afterwards:

i) pushups & situps
ii) the military chest press
iii) biceps curls with weights to improve your arms
iv) beach running to improve your legs
v) aerobics classes to improve your heart & lungs
vi) triceps pressdowns, squats

Part III: THE CHARACTER *More Journal Writing*

Congratulations! You are on Day 9 of the MegaLiving! program and are now on the way to becoming the very best that you can be. The fact that you have come this far confirms that you are among the minority of people who have the discipline to persist with things in order to achieve self-mastery. Write for five minutes in your journal all the benefits you have noticed and all that you have learned about personal power and your own positive qualities over the past 8 days. List your weaknesses as well: those thoughts that are preventing true happiness, those bad habits that are denying you the bountiful life that you are now certain is yours and those factors in your life which you must change.

Day 10

Date:_____

Part I: THE MIND   *The Power of the Book: Readers are Leaders!*

One of, if not the most important thing you can do for mastery of yourself is incredibly easy: read something inspiring and valuable every day. Reading can take you to new heights as knowledge truly is power. Reading will give you brilliant ideas on how to improve every aspect of your life. The key is to surround yourself with such thoughts so you are literally forced to think positively and to accept no limitations.

All the mistakes of this world have already been made and their solutions appear in books. Is there really any point in making them again? The trick in life is to make it easier, not harder and the habit of reading will certainly do this for you. Start your own personal excellence library and make the following ten books its foundation:

  i)   *Think and Grow Rich,* Napoleon Hill
  ii)   *Unlimited Power,* Anthony Robbins
  iii)   *The Power of the Subconscious Mind,* Dr. Joseph Murphy
  iv)   *The Power of Positive Thinking,* Rev. Norman Vincent Peale
  v)   *Life's Little Instruction Book,* Jackson Brown Jr.
  vi)   *The Story of My Experiments with Truth,* Mahatma Ghandi
  vii)   *Fit For Life,* Harvey Diamond
  viii)   *Thoughts on the Business of Life,* Forbes
  ix)   *Maximum Achievement,* Brian Tracy
  x)   *The Magic of Believing,* Claude Bristol

Part II: THE BODY   *Stop Acting Your Age- The Importance of Good Posture*

If you act old you will be old. Why buy into the myth that you must age according to a certain schedule and process. Why not resolve to beat age and live a youthful, passionate existence? The first step is to physically act young. Improve your posture, ensuring that your back is straight. This will also allow you to breathe properly.

Also, take purposeful steps and do not walk like an old person. The essence of youthful living is to prevent an elderly person from moving into your body and you can do so by living young.

Part III: THE CHARACTER   *Broadening Your Worldview*

One of the most beneficial things you can do for yourself is to travel the world. Travelling shows you what the world is like and, importantly, how very lucky you are. In the heat of everyday life, we tend to let the little things take on a much greater importance than they should. Who cares if the paper came late today or if the boss was in a bad mood? Do you have food on your table? Are you living in a state of war? Learning about the world, even through reading if you cannot travel, will put things into perspective and ensure that you realize all of the gifts life has bestowed on you. Do not waste another minute worrying about the small troubles and past events. You are more than this and today is the day to rise to the heights that you are certainly capable of living at.

Day 11

Part I: THE MIND   *The Master Blaster Technique for Personal Excellence*

A highly positive self-image is essential for mastery of your mind, body and character. Every moment of every hour of everyday, you must guard against thinking limiting thoughts that damage your self-image. Once you start thinking such thoughts (i.e. I am not intelligent, charismatic etc.), they will soon become habit forming and seriously affect your performance in life.

A very valuable technique to rid yourself of any negative self images is the Master Blaster. Write down a list of all the negative qualities you believe that you have. Now find a quiet place and get into a very deep state of relaxation (perhaps by deep breathing or by some of the other strategies you have learned in this book).

Once you are relaxed, picture the negative self image and quality (i.e., if it is overeating and obesity, picture yourself gorging at a meal and being overweight). Now make the image in your mind's eye clearer- really see it. Now, most importantly, visualize two sticks of dynamite being placed at both ends of the picture and with the lighting of a match watch the negative self-image explode into a hundred million tiny pieces. See the image shattered! Now immediately replace the old image with a bright, clear, big one of the quality you desire to have or the way you wish to look. Repeat the entire process at least 20 times on the first try and then about 5 times a day for the next 21 days. Your self-image will dramatically improve with this very special exercise.

Part II: THE BODY   *Sticking with Your Exercise Program*

Over the past 10 days, you should have been doing at least 20 minutes of exercise every day. If you are not fit, gentle walks through the woods or swimming would be just fine. If you are fortunate enough to be in shape, you should have been doing more than 20 minutes and pushing yourself towards the higher levels you are capable of achieving.

One of your most important life habits should be to exercise vigorously at least four or five times a week. If you can do it everyday without straining your body all the better. Such physical conditioning keeps you young, aids in your digestion and general health and significantly improves your energy reserves. No more excuses, take Nike's advice and "**Just Do It!**"

Part III: THE CHARACTER   *Purging Your World of Worries*

It is tremendously important to have a relaxed, serene mind. A calm mind will do wonders for you and lead to a strong, vital body. A mind free of worries and negative thoughts must be your first priority if you want a truly happy life. Like most other things, a positive, winning mindset can be cultivated through practice.

Exercise: Make a list of every single thing that is worrying you . List your loans, any challenges at work, health troubles -everything. The very act of writing out the list is most beneficial and freeing. Once you have listed everything you can think of, from the smallest worry to the biggest, rip up the list into as many pieces as possible and see your worries crumble into the dustbin. Bruce Lee, the martial arts legend, used a similar technique to free himself of any negative thoughts.

Day 12

Date:_____

Part I: THE MIND   *Building a Routine for Mental Toughness*

You are at the stage of this program where you have learned the strategies for success practised by the great citizens of this world. Meditation, focusing, deep breathing and visualization techniques have now become part of your success arsenal. The key is to develop a routine so that you use them daily to ensure that you stay at the very top of your game. Set aside at least 30-45 minutes every morning to attend to your personal development, the earlier the better. Get into the following routine:

      i)   *5 minutes: Ask yourself 5 Questions for Success.*
          -What will I do to make today a masterpiece? (picture it)
          -What am I grateful for? (list everything)
          -What will I improve today?
          -Who will I serve today?
          -What will make me laugh today?

      ii)   *15 minutes: Get into a serene mindset by meditating*

Meditation is practised by a tremendous number of superachievers and it has now gone mainstream. Do not fear that it is something done by the flowerchildren of the '60s and is not for you. Elite athletes use it for peak performance and so should you. Nothing calms your overworked mind better. Practise focusing on a flower or pleasant object for 15 minutes. Think of nothing else. Build up the muscle of your mind so that you are in total control and think only of the object. Over the weeks, you will notice that the little thoughts that used to ruin your mood and distract you can be expelled from your mind instantly.

      iii)   *10 minutes: Get inspired to seize this day!*

"Happiness is not a state to arrive at but a manner of travelling" said Margaret Runbeck. This is so very true and every second of your life must be happy. The trick is to surround yourself with happy thoughts and things. Here is a huge secret: happiness is a habit. Happiness is not something which develops because you win the lottery or get a great job. Some of the world's happiest people are its poorest or ones that have endured tremendous hardship. But they developed the habit of looking for the positive in everything. Surround yourself with inspirational books, tapes and pictures. For 10 minutes, at the very least, read a dynamic book that will supercharge your spirit.

Part II: THE BODY   *Goal Review*

Review your physical goals from Day 1. Are you doing something each day to move towards them? Keep planning your attack and write out inspiring notes to yourself aimed at attaining your goals.

Part III: THE CHARACTER   *Fun Exercise*

Today's exercise is easy. Rent *It's A Wonderful World* (Jimmy Stewart) from the videostore and watch it tonight. What does it teach you and what secrets for success have you learned?

Day 13

Part I: THE MIND   *Mental Racewalking*

Over & over, this program has emphasized that your mind can be sharpened and strengthened to perform things that you have never believed possible. You can increase your peace of mind, concentration powers, will-power, memory and creativity, among other things, by training.

One of the most effective ways to charge up your mind so that you will excel at some mental activity (i.e. a project at work or an important essay at school) is Mental Racewalking. The way to warm up the mind for peak mental performance is to speed it up. Do the following exercise:

> Mental racewalking: Pick up a newspaper or a magazine. Select any noun in any article (i.e. health in the Health Section). Now for 5 minutes, *as quickly as possible and without stopping* write down everything that your mind associates with the word "health". After 5 minutes, relax for a minute by deep breathing and move on to your project or essay.

Part II: THE BODY   *Nutritional Excellence*

To get the most out of life and to have the energy to do all the things that you have now been motivated to do, you must be very careful of what you put into your body. Bad foods will slow you down, effect your moods and keep you from perfect health. A diet high in fruits & vegetables will keep you strong, energetic and highly vital.

Today, take 15 minutes and list all the things you have eaten over the past 2 days. If you cannot remember, list the things you generally eat. Notice all the high fat offenders like whole milk products, fried foods, snack foods, creamy salad dressings, pastries and cheeses. Eliminate 25% of these this week alone. This will not be as hard as it sounds given all the low-fat alternatives at your grocery store. For example, low-fat cheese, milk and meats are available everywhere.

Also, follow these powerful tips for health excellence:

      i)   Stop overeating. Eat only what you need & push the rest away.
      ii)   Have as much fresh fruit as you can in the morning.
     iii)   Do not eat anything after 8pm
     iv)   Eat a salad with every meal (it will help your digestion and increase your energy level significantly). Also, cut down on your meat intake.

Part III: THE CHARACTER   *Manage Your Time!*

Time is one of the most precious commodities you have. We have 168 hours in a week. How much of this time are you wasting? 2 hours of TV a night is 14 hours a week. This is a full day of time that you could have spent building up your health, enriching your relationships, writing that book you have always talked about or taking a new initiative at work that would make you the standout you know you are. Stop wasting time!

Make a list of all the time wasters in your life that are sucking away your productivity. Stop gossiping on the phone, hanging out at the coffee room and focus on the things that are really important to achieving your dreams. The minute lost is gone forever.

Day 14

Part I: THE MIND   *Break All the Rules!*

The superachievers of this world, those people that live each second to the maximum and are living their dreams have one thing in common: they accept no limitations on what they can have from this life. You too must shatter the rules about what you can become, what you can do with your life, the rules about the health that you must have and the limits on the fun in your day. Why can't you become a millionaire, sail around the Caribbean, travel to Bali, write a bestselling novel, run a marathon or learn to fly? Change your mindset today. Start getting exposed to the people of this world who have done these things with much less ability than you have. If someone says you are too old to start your own business, think otherwise. If someone says you are not fit enough to become a competitive runner, train harder than ever and show them that they know nothing about who you are. Become a MegaLiver! today.

Exercise: ***Dreaming For Personal Excellence***

Make a list of the top 10 dreams that you have. Be creative and the more fun the better. List only those things you really want to have happen. Now think, emotionally, about what it would feel like if those dreams came true. What would your family say and how would it improve your life. Next, write out one thing you will do over the next week, no matter how small, to get on the path for attaining your dreams. If your goal is sailing to the Bahamas, sign up for sailing lessons tomorrow-DO IT! If your goal is to start a business, look for one of the many seminars available on the subject and go to it. Meet others who want to do the same thing for ideas, inspiration and motivation. Take some action every single day to move towards your dreams. If you really want them to come true, if you really want to have all that is yours, start today, not ten years from today.

Part II: THE BODY   *Physical Conditioning- The Next Level*

"First say to yourself what you would be and then do what you have to do" wrote Emerson. In Day 1 of the MegaLiving! program you committed yourself to achieving certain physical goals. You should now be on the path towards them. Everything is about habit and you should now be into the habit of exercise, even if only for 20 minutes a day. Exercise is the secret fountain of youth. It is so very simple to do and the benefits are enormous. Keep up your routine. If possible, take your physical conditioning to a higher level today. Run just a little faster, swim just a little longer or walk up that long hill you have avoided climbing for the past 2 weeks.

Part III: THE CHARACTER   *Life Tips*

i)   Be the most enthusiastic person you know. Be kind, be strong and be serene.
ii)   Act youthful, live with an air of fun, laugh hard, laugh often.
iii)   Go to bed early and wake up before 6 am. Pray.
iv)   Be humble, save 10% of your income every month and give something to charity yearly.
v)   Control your emotions and never get angry. Count to 10 if you feel anger coming.
vi)   Associate with positive, active and loving people.
vii)   Eat moderately, eat light food and have a balanced diet.
viii)   Be honest in everything you do. Be noble & courteous to all. Guard your reputation.
ix)   Fast once a month, taking mild fruits only. It is very cleansing .
x)   Achieve your dreams, think big but keep it simple.

Day 15

Date:_____

Part I: THE MIND   *More Affirmations for Excellence*

Autosuggestion will make things happen for you. Any thought, when constantly repeated affects the powerful subconscious mind. Once the thought is accepted, your will is then directed towards the accomplishment of the goal. This technique, however strange it might seem, has been used with tremendous success for many years. Napoleon Hill, the man who studied hundreds of America's most successful people, urged it on his readers in *Think and Grow Rich*. The strategy works so make it a tool for your personal mastery. Below are 6 of the most effective affirmations which you should repeat to yourself throughout the day (it is essential for you to say the affirmation with great emotion and belief in its truth):

> i)   "I am serene, strong & happy"
> ii)   "I have everything I want in this world & am grateful"
> iii)   "Every day, I get better & better"
> iv)   "Wealth-Success"
> v)   "I have tremendous energy & vitality"
> vi)   "I am young, healthy & tranquil"

Part II: THE BODY   *Boosting Your Longevity*

Over the next 15 days, incorporate the following powerful longevity tips into your life:

> i)   After age 50, your oil glands start to slow down. It is key that you keep your skin looking youthful and supple by using a moisturizer containing lanolin or the oils of coconut, safflower or wheat germ. Use it right after you get out of the shower.

> ii)   Try using Retin-A. This is the so-called youth ingredient that reduces age lines on your face. The prescription cream encourages the growth of new skin proteins, blood vessels and speeds the removal of dead skin cells.

> iii)   A regular weight training plan when combined with aerobic activity will make you look years younger.

> iv)   Take a brisk walk every day. In a study of 16, 936 Harvard Alumni, those who engaged in physical activity clearly had lower death rates.

Part III: THE CHARACTER   *Enthusiasm*

"Nothing great was ever achieved without enthusiasm" said Ralph Waldo Emerson whilst Twain attributed the secret of his success to the fact that "I was born excited." In survey after survey, leaders say that enthusiasm is key for success. To develop enthusiasm you must figure out what fires your soul. You don't have to sit chained to a desk from 9 to 5 every day. Determine what it is you love to do and then do it. The passion which comes from doing that which you love creates enthusiasm. Today, put an elastic band around your wrist. This is "the band of enthusiasm." Today and every day after, you must be the most enthusiastic person you know. The band will remind you of the many benefits of enthusiasm and of your commitment to be enthusiastic and zestful throughout this wonderful day.

Day 16

Date:_____

Part I: THE MIND   *The Mini-Vacation*

It is essential, if you are to meet with true self-mastery, that you remove all tension from your body. Too much stress impedes performance and prevents you from tapping the huge potential lying dormant inside of you. Stress reduction exercises must become a part of your daily routine and will only take a few minutes of your time. Once you start using them, you will feel much calmer, stronger and happy.

EXERCISE: Sit down in a quiet place and get very comfortable. If you are in your office, shut the door and hold all calls. Shut your eyes and start breathing deeply. Inhale deeply watching the belly move out like a big balloon. Hold the breath and then exhale fully. In your mind's eye, see all your worries and tension flooding out of you like a chimney spewing out smoke. Keep breathing deeply for 2 minutes, each time feeling yourself becoming more and more relaxed. Focus only on the breathing, nothing else.

Now, starting with your feet, feel that your body is getting incredibly heavy. Your ankles are sinking towards the floor with the weight. Then feel your legs loosening up, see the muscles relaxing and all tension vanishing. Move up through the torso, arms, neck and head. You will now feel exceptionally relaxed. Now imagine you are on vacation. You have all the time in the world. You have no watch and no appointments. You find yourself barefoot in a lush, green forest. Hear the birds chirping and the bubbling brook in the distance. Smell the wild roses and lavender in the bushes. As you walk, feel the moist earth against your soles. See the sunlight peaking through the trees at certain places, warming up that particular area as you walk by. You walk through this stunningly green forest to a lake. The lake is stiller than a plate of glass and you study the reflections the trees make on the surface of the water. Your mind is as tranquil as this lake. You feel deeply calm and at one with nature. This is your mini-vacation. Enjoy it. Now open your eyes & go back to work, refreshed, relaxed and alive.

Part II: THE BODY   *Banishing Your Belly*

Strong abdominal muscles are very important for peak health. As we get older, it becomes more & more difficult to keep the stomach toned and lean. The trick to a taut stomach is to lose the fat by aerobic exercise, build the muscle below the surface by weight training or sit-ups and keep the stomach thin by eating a light diet with low-fat foods. Each day for the next 14, do 20 sit-ups.

Part III: THE CHARACTER   *Becoming a Better Lover*

If you want to be a chef, you do not simply walk into a kitchen and say you are a chef. You must train. If you want to be a teacher, you don't walk into the classroom and start to teach, you train. In the same vein, you were not born a lover. To get the most out of your relationships and really love those around you, you must train and work at being a great lover. On a piece of paper, write out those people you want to become closer to, those people you really want to love. Now, write out a "love letter" to each one of these people. You will not send it so be as expressive and open as possible. Really tell them how you feel and what you think of them. Be romantic, be creative, be silly but be sincere. The very act of writing these love letters is very fulfilling and will tap your "love skills" which will now emerge to provide you with more enriching relationships. Finally, take some action to improve these relationships this week.

Day 17

Date:_____

Part I: THE MIND   *Revisiting Kaizen: Constant & Never Ending Improvement*

This book has emphasized the importance of kaizen: daily improvement in all aspects of your life. The very fact that you are doing this program and have come this far shows that you are a breed apart from the average person who believes that things cannot be changed and they must accept the deck that life has dealt them. Each and every day, take a step, no matter how small to improve yourself. This is the essence of MegaLiving! If you take such steps daily, the results will start to become more and more noticeable until they snowball and every aspect of your life moves to a higher level. Here are a few suggestions for using the principle of kaizen today:

i)	Start your memoirs
ii)	Unplug your TV & really communicate to those around you
iii)	Write 5 letters to old friends (a wonderful habit!)
iv)	Finish everything you start today
v)	Stretch yourself & do something gutsy!
vi)	Sign up for a language course, take jazz trumpet lessons, watch Letterman
vii)	Read 3 different newspapers today & write to the editor
viii)	Go to the opera tonight, the symphony or the ballet - explore life!
ix)	Listen to the radio, review your financial goals, dream
x)	Visualize the person you are determined to become

Part II: THE BODY   *Energizing Yourself*

You will not reach your goals without energy. Ghandi slept 4 hours a night. He had both the energy and the desire to lead his country to independence. Here are some of the best strategies for increasing your energy levels (select 2 to incorporate into your daily routine):

i)	Be active. Paradoxically, you'll have more energy if you expend it.
ii)	Use the deep breathing techniques in this book.
iii)	Eat energizing foods: fresh fruits & vegetables
iv)	Nothing drains energy more than worrying. Relax, meditate & loosen up.
v)	Use autosuggestion: repeat "I am totally juiced up and energetic!"
vi)	Take a brisk walk after dinner, if only for 10 minutes
vii)	Listen to your favorite music that has charged you up in the past
viii)	Take a power-nap if you are tired (15 minutes maximum)

Part III: THE CHARACTER   *More Journal Writing*

Take out your success journal & write out in a detailed way all the changes you are noticing in your thoughts and in your life. What positive things are happening to you? What challenges are you still facing and what will you do to overcome them and reach all the goals you set for yourself on Day 1? List the strategies and ideas you have learned to date from the MegaLiving! program. Now congratulate yourself for getting this far and moving closer to the Perfect Life that is yours.

Day 18

Date:_____

Part I: THE MIND   *The Power of Music*

"Music has charms to soothe a savage beast" wrote the English poet William Congreve. Music can be used to ensure that your mindset remains serene and focused. People are only now starting to realize the many wonderful effects music has on our moods. Many Olympic athletes are using music as part of their training regimen. You can make it a part of yours.

When you wish to enter a state of tranquility, classical music works best. Pieces such as Pachelbel's Canon are incredibly soothing and will transport you to another world. Set aside a time, perhaps after dinner, to sit down and concentrate fully on the music. Let it enter your soul and work its charms. Jazz music also works wonders and provides a lift to your spirit keeping it soaring and inspired. If you don't want to go out and buy this music, simply listen to the many classical and jazz stations on your radio. Radio is excellent and enjoy its many benefits.

Part II: THE BODY   *Think Healthy -Be Healthy*

Many doctors are now recognizing that our thoughts affect our immune system and our general health. Emotional states such as fear and sadness are processed in the limbic system and hypothalamus which then sends signals to the body's immune system via chemicals called neuropeptides. The current philosophy argues that a mental image of a healthy body can be communicated from the brain to the immune system's cells which act in such a fashion so as to duplicate the mental image that was held in the mind.

Cancer patients have effectively used creative visualization and imagery exercises to picture immune cells killing the cancerous ones, sometimes with startling results. You can use this strategy for maintaining a state of perfect health. Simply get yourself into a relaxed state of mind using one of the calming techniques you have learned. Then, in a detailed way, picture yourself in a perfect state physically. See your skin glow and your face looking healthy. See yourself as lean, energetic and happy. Do this exercise twice a day for the next few months and you will reap positive rewards in your self-esteem as well as in your general health condition.

Part III: THE CHARACTER   *The Ideal Person*

Practise the 6 virtues of the Ideal Person:

    i)   Self-mastery in all situations
    ii)   Self-control of all of the senses
    iii)   Control in diet and soberness
    iv)   Self-command of temper and desires
    v)   Humility in success, hope in defeat
    vi)   Compassion to all, moderation in life & persistence in goals

---

Day 19

Date:_____

Part I: THE MIND   *Tapping Your Creativity*

It is essential that you develop your mental creativity muscles. With enhanced creativity, you will get all sorts of ideas to help you in your quest for personal excellence and the Perfect Life. Creativity will also make your life more playful, joyous and rewarding.

First get into a relaxed frame of mind for today's exercise. A new technique you may use is to shut your eyes and vividly picture a blackboard. Gradually, words start to appear on the board and as you look closer you see your name with the word "relax" next to it, all the way down the long blackboard. Study the blackboard and clearly see these words on it.

Now , with your eyes still shut, picture yourself as you were when you were a 6 year old child. What likes did you have and what things did you do for fun. Tap the happy, creative and lively child sleeping inside of you. How did you see adults then? What pranks did you play? Visualize all of this and make it fun. For the rest of today, see things as a child might. Shake up your perspective. At the office or in your home, stand on a chair and see what it looks like up there. Do something you have never done like visiting an art gallery or riding a roller coaster. Focus on being creative and playful in the things you do. You will never be the same!

Part II: THE BODY   *More Exercise*

Your exercise program should be well underway and part of your daily routine. You must now have started to see and feel the powerful results that this simple activity can bring. Today, in your journal, write down 5 benefits of exercise. Then, from a magazine or the newspaper, find a picture of someone with the physical condition that you want to have. Get a hero or a role model and tape it to your bathroom mirror or even better, to the fridge. Look at it regularly and focus on developing such a shape.

Part III: THE CHARACTER   *Becoming a Leader*

Start to develop the 10 Master Keys to Leadership:

i)	Belief in your dreams
ii)	Courage and supreme persistence
iii)	Enthusiasm
iv)	Consideration for others
v)	Self-control and self-mastery
vi)	Well-developed social skills and diplomacy
vii)	The habit of doing far more than expected
viii)	Long-term planning & organization
ix)	Calculated risk taking
x)	A burning desire to succeed & faith in success

Day 20

Part I: THE MIND   *Raising Your Standards*

Today make a decision that will surely change your life: raise your standards. Raise the level of what you expect of yourself, the way you treat your body, the thoughts you put into your mind and the way you live your life. Do not accept mediocrity. Give up being a member of the pack. Commit yourself to true life excellence. Be the very best you can be and start giving 110% in every single area of your life from your relationships to your professional activities.

Here are the 5 Keys to making excellence your life-standard:

   i)   **Change your attitude**. Most successful people have an attitude which prevents them from being anything but the best.

   ii)   **Get in the habit of being outstanding**. Once you make small steps each day to confirm your new standard of working, playing and living, there will be no going back after a few months. MegaLiving! will be your habit.

   iii) **Publicize your new standards to those closest to you**. Get some pressure on yourself to ensure that you do not budge from your commitment to living every moment of life to the fullest and making it a true masterpiece.

   iv)   **Remember your "old self."** Anytime you think of the bad habits that you are changing or the past standards that you once lived by, proudly tell yourself that that was the way you *were- that was the old you &* *you will never go back.*

   v)   **Try to get others to raise their standards with you**. We all can explode our limitations in a second if we make the simple decision to do so.

Part II: THE BODY   *Serene Body= Serene Mind*

It has been emphasized throughout the MegaLiving! program that it is essential that you develop a serene, relaxed mindset which will guarantee your success as a peak performer. This comes with practise and you have learned exercises to dramatically enhance your concentration & focus. Stand guard at the gates of your mind and be so mentally tough that not even one negative thought enters your superbly conditioned mind. Today, take Day 16's mini-vacation and practise this serenity technique every day for the next nine.

Part III: THE CHARACTER

Take 20 minutes tonight & pull out you success journal. Jot down the first 25 things you want out of life. Anything you have ever dreamed of should be there. If it is sailing to Hawaii, put it down. Now, using deep breathing and any one of the relaxation strategies you have learned in this book (i.e. the mini-vacation is a good one), get into a very relaxed state. Feel any tension & worrying thoughts leave your mind like clouds moving out of a blue sky to make way for the radiant sunshine. Once you feel serene, visualize yourself doing all the things you dreamed of & having all the possessions you wrote down. Become aware of what you want, then act on the dreams.

Day 21

Date:_____

Your Day Off!   **Enjoy the Rewards of MegaLiving!**

Congratulations are due to you today! You have reached Day 21 of the MegaLiving! Program & are on the golden road to a Perfect Life filled with pure joy, peak health, happy relationships, excitement, success and contentment. You have powerfully shown yourself what you can do and the potential within you to achieve your dreams. By reaching Day 21, you are amongst a minority of people who have the discipline to start and stay with this revolutionary personal excellence program for the long run.

Over the 3 weeks you have been practising MegaLiving!, changes have taken place in every area of your life. You have looked at all of the aspects of your world and taken positive steps to change what you don't like. You have taken actions that will pay huge dividends to you. New habits are starting to take root. New ideas about what you will contribute to this world are dancing in your mind. You have more energy, confidence & zest for life. In a word, you are "Mega Living!"

You have worked hard to get to this stage of the program. It was not easy and you have made some sacrifices. But you are here and you are outstanding! Today is your day off. Do something adventurous, fun or silly. Be like a kid for the day, curious and enthusiastic. Walk along the ocean or see that play you have missed so often. Before you dash off to maximize your day off, quickly run through the brief assessment below to let you know where you stand with MegaLiving! and where you must place your focus to reach your goals.

MegaLiving! Assessment

	Good-Very Good	*Excellent- Outstanding*
Mental Conditioning		
Physical Conditioning		
Character Building		
Motivation Level		
Self-Happiness Rating		

Day 22

Date:_____

Part I: THE MIND   *Don't Believe in Defeat*

Combine a powerful faith in the incredible abilities that lie deep inside of you with guts, determination and enthusiasm and you will succeed in every challenge you come up against. You should now be using the 5 Questions of Success that you learned in Day 3 of the program. The first one is, of course, "How can I make today a living Masterpiece?" To make each moment of every glorious day a masterpiece, it is essential to have a tremendous belief in yourself and in the goals you have committed yourself to realizing. Challenges and obstacles will appear, this is reality. But you can turn them around. See them as opportunities and chances to grow and develop further. Make problems a game. Ask what wisdom will you gain from them, how will they make you stronger and tougher and what will happen if you allow them to seep into your winning mindset. Believe in your unlimited potential. Believe in your tremendous personal power. Believe in yourself.

Part II: THE BODY   *How to Take a Walk*

Walking is excellent nutrition for the mind. It creates calmness, happiness and wholeness. In this high-pressure world, we forget about the truly simple pleasure of a long walk through the forest or a brisk walk along the waterfront. You may not have access to posh country clubs, expensive golf resorts or private fitness facilities but you can walk. The MegaLiving! Program has emphasized over and over the tremendous importance of exercising daily. This should now be one of your life habits. The treat of a walk on a regular basis should never be forgotten.

5 Suggestions on Taking Walks (a wonderful pleasure):

i)   Find a lovely, natural place. Even the busiest city has one.
ii) Walk alone and at a quiet time of the day (early a.m. is great)
iii) Remove from your mind all worldly cares. Focus only on the walk
iv) Breath deeply & enjoy the air, scents, scenery and soulful quiet
v)   Walk strongly, with good posture and balanced steps

Part III: THE CHARACTER   *10 Golden Keys to Popularity*

i)   Remember people's names. It is the sweetest sound they know.
ii)   Smile often, laugh often. Know 3 great, clean jokes.
iii)   Become a great listener. Use the 70/30 Rule. Listen 70% of the time, talk only 30%.
iv)   Perfect your manners. They are a mark of true polish and character.
v)   Do small, kind gestures for people every day. Make every day count.
vi)   Never say someone is wrong. Don't argue. If you don't agree, keep quiet.
vii)   Inspire people, encourage people and befriend people.
viii) Develop your contacts. Write letters often and make phone calls.
ix)   Be the most honest person you know.
x)   Give more than you receive. It always comes back in a river.

Day 23

Date:_____

Part I: THE MIND   *More Memory Conditioning*

You have learned that you have a photographic memory sleeping in your mind. Details you thought had vanished have been retained and are awaiting the conditioning of your memory. Tap its real potential.

The memory is like every other muscle, you must use it or lose it. Get in the habit of using it. Stop making grocery lists, use you memory. Picture the ten items you need. See yourself at the grocery store picking every one of the items up and inspecting them. Make up a colorful, vivid story using the things you need so you will be certain to get everything. Start memorizing a paragraph of poetry or literature every day. Turn off that television set and spend a half hour on your greatest possession: your limitless mind.

Part II: THE BODY   *More Exercising*

The bountiful benefits of physical conditioning should be showing up now. It has been over 3 weeks of exercise and you must feel more energetic, confident and healthy. Little digestive or skin problems which may have plagued you in the past should have cleared up. Getting out of bed will be easier and your enthusiasm level is skyrocketing. Today, increase the level of your exercise program. Work out longer, run faster, swim harder. Do it! Do it! Do it!

Part III: THE CHARACTER   *Mastery of Problems*

The MegaLiving! program has shown you that the quality of your life is the quality of your communication (with others and, most importantly, yourself). The way you interpret events determines your happiness and your level of success. Your attitude determines your altitude. Once you have developed a winner's mindset, nothing will stop you.

Problems will always crop up. The peak performer uses them as learning experiences and motivators to work harder and accomplish more. One of the best strategies for neutralizing the possible negative effects of problems is to ask yourself questions. Asking yourself questions puts things into perspective, focuses your mind on the positive elements of what has happened and prevents your energy from being drained by worry.

A Secret for Mastering Life's Problems Quickly

The next time you are faced with one of life's little problems, *on a piece of paper*, ask yourself the following questions:

i)	How can this experience help me? What lesson have I learned?
ii)	What will happen if I let this defeat me & if I worry?
iii)	What can I do to ensure that this never happens again?
iv)	What can I do to enjoy this situation & even laugh about it?
v)	What am I grateful for?

Day 24

Date:_____

Part I: THE MIND   *Eliminating Your Fears Forever*

Emerson has said "do the thing you fear and the death of fear is certain." Lasting life-mastery and personal success will only happen when you directly attack those obstacles which may have held you back in the past. The first step is to eliminate your fears once and for all.

The Master Blaster technique you learned earlier (Day 11) is an excellent tool to blast fears out of your mind. Really, the technique is nothing more than simple conditioning of the mind to enjoy the thing you were once afraid of or felt negative towards. Today, make a list of the fears which have prevented you from being the best you can be. The first stage is to be clearly aware of them, the second is to take concrete actions to eliminate them. Do you fear public speaking, meeting people, making huge amounts of money, taking new risks or making important changes? Note your fears. Then, under each one, make an action plan to do the very thing you fear more often.

If you fear speaking, offer to give 3 presentations over the coming months to your colleagues at work. Also, start reading every book you can get on public speaking. Take a course on the subject and develop a burning desire to be the very best speaker you know. Join Toastmasters and find some good role models who will gladly share their secrets of success with you. Post pictures of Churchill and other powerful orators over your bed and surround yourself with positive motivators which will guarantee your success. Each time a fearful thought enters your mind, replace it immediately and forcefully with a mental picture of you as a fiery, dynamic speaker. Work hard over the next week to identify all of your other fears, no matter how small. Attack them with a vengeance. You will be surprised how quickly they will disappear.

Part II: THE BODY   *The Business of Living a Long Time*

Throughout this program, your have received secrets to live longer and healthier. The key is to really have a powerful belief in your personal vitality and understand that you really are only as old as you think you are. Today, in a quiet moment, picture yourself as you hope to be in 2, 10, 20 and 30 years. Drive home to yourself that your body has incredible potential for youthfulness and vigor. Now that you are exercising, eating more fruits and vegetables & less meat, relaxing your mind and body daily , thinking positively and living correctly, you are on the path to real longevity. Every day, even for a minute, say to yourself "I am youthful, dynamic and vital." Visualize yourself as energetic and young with a glowing complexion and a toned physique. Everything is created twice -first in the mind and then outside of it.

Part III: THE CHARACTER   *Respect & Character*

It has been said that knowledge will give you power but character will give you respect. You have been exposed to some of the world's most significant tools for personal development in the MegaLiving! 30 day program for self-mastery. You have the knowledge, now build your character. Each day for the past 23, you have consistently taken steps to become more confident, motivated and vital. Make a "strong as rock" character one of your most important goals. Set your goals and values high and never move away from them. Live a life of integrity and truth. Live with passion and live honorably. Believe in yourself and your human potential!

Day 25

Date:_____

Part I: THE MIND   *Suggestive Articulation (More Mantras for Mastery)*

Words undoubtedly have profound suggestive power. What we think and say all day becomes our reality. You can develop great serenity by getting into a relaxed state and repeating "tranquility" to yourself over and over. You can develop mental toughness by quietly repeating "I am tough, I am powerful" to yourself all the way to work every morning. Words influence the subconscious mind which is the seat of enormous personal power-never underestimate its abilities.

Today, rid yourself of all the little negative sayings you accidentally use throughout the day. Stop saying "I've always been terrible with names" or "I've never had much energy in the morning." If you make these kinds of harmful statements, you can bet you will never remember names and always be groggy every morning. Sit down and clearly identify any phrases you regularly use which undermine your true potential for life mastery and get them out of your vocabulary.

Mastery Mantras

i) For Energy: "I am active and love to achieve." Now take action today, be alive!
ii) For Perfect Health: "I am incredibly healthy & vital, I feel so fit today."
iii) For Wealth: "I am wealthy, I have real success."

Part II: THE BODY   *Stress Reducer*

After your workout today, treat yourself to a stress reducer. Book a professional massage or give yourself one (see technique from Day 4). Try an acupuncture treatment or a sauna/whirlpool. Try anything new but give yourself a relaxing treat as a reward for your excellent efforts at physical conditioning.

Part III: THE CHARACTER   *More Readings - Knowledge is Power*

On Day 10, you were exposed to a number of books that should form the core of your library of personal mastery books. Most of them are very inexpensive but actually of priceless value. Today, read for one hour, *at the very least*, from Napoleon Hill's superb book *Think and Grow Rich*. This book will surely have a very great impact on you and put you on the road to personal and financial abundance.

When you have finished your reading, take out your success journal and write down Napoleon Hill's 13 Principles. Study them and picture vividly how you could put them to use in your life. Now set your goal as he suggests and take active steps to make certain that you are on your way to achieving this dream. Over then next week, finish the book and make notes on its key points so that you have them on your fingertips.

Day 26

Date:_____

Part I: THE MIND *Surround Yourself By Excellence*

You have now propelled yourself to a new level of focus and positivity. The key is to now ensure that every thought that enters your mind is a good one & a motivating one. To do this, start listening to tapes of the great positive thinkers of this world such as Reverend Norman Vincent Peale, read the books of Emerson and Carnegie, learn the stories of those with much less than you who achieved life mastery. Stop wasting time thinking about what is missing in your life and start dreaming and achieving your ultimate goals.

Also, surround yourself with other triggers for happiness in your life. When you wake up, play some soulful jazz or serenely pleasant classical music. Associate with only those who are inspired by life and who refuse to accept anything but the very best that this dazzling world has to offer. Keep adding to your success library, go to seminars on mastery of your character, life and virtues. Live by the Kaizen principle of daily and constant improvement. Make this your personal trademark.

Part II: THE BODY *Fasting For Health & Energy*

For thousands of years, people have fasted. Going without food for a day or at least restricting your diet to fruits and juices for a day will cleanse your system, give you more energy and significantly increase your self-control. It is a technique to try once every month for general health maintenance. Consult your physician if you have a health problem prior to fasting.
Today, plan to fast for one day over the next 2 weeks. Schedule this and stick to your commitment. Your discipline muscles are getting stronger & stronger every day. Keep it up, self-control does wonders for you life!

Part III: THE CHARACTER *The Wonders of Listening*

One of the most essential qualities of an outstanding individual is the ability to listen to others intently. In our fast-paced, egocentric world, we are often too self-centered to take the time to listen to others, even those we love the most. But once we start listening to those we are surrounded by, we learn things we never knew before. People who once appeared boring suddenly have valuable insights from which you can learn and grow. As well, once you start developing the powerful listening habit, your relationships start to improve. You start to see the point of view of others and develop more compassion and understanding. People start enjoying your company even more and your personal contacts dramatically increase. The art of listening must be cultivated. Here are some strategies to become the best listener you know:

  i)   **Stop talking so much.** Use your self-control to start listening more today

 ii)   **Visualize being the world's best listener.** In the morning, focus for a
         couple of minutes on your excellent ability to listen and how you plan to
         use this skill in your meetings today.

iii)   **Stop interrupting others.** We all do it. Start a game & pay your friends
         or family members a dollar each time you cut them off.

Day 27

Date:_____

Part I: THE MIND   *The Magic of Silence*

This is a fast-paced world we live in. We can thrive on the chaos by developing strategies to ensure that we remain the calm within the eye of the storm. The habit of inner serenity is tremendously important for personal excellence. This morning, appreciate the power of silence. Silence provides a tonic for even the most anxious mind and returns one to a state of tranquility. Take half an hour out of your morning schedule and sit in the quietest place in your home. Now focus on the silence, enjoying the peace. You will feel like getting up and doing something after only a few minutes but muster up all the self-control you have developed through this program and resist the urge. Simply be still. Listen to your heartbeat or feel the weight of your head on your shoulders. You will start to notice things you have never seen before when you are silent and internally still. Make the enjoyment of silence an integral part of your life routine.

Part II: THE BODY   *Making Exercise a Delight*

Former President Ronald Reagan once stated one of the true keys to success in physical conditioning: "find something you enjoy and keep the exercise varied." You have been doing something physically challenging for the past 26 days of the MegaLiving! program. You have taken your energy levels and conditioning to a much higher level and are starting to see positive changes in all areas of your life. Do not let boredom set in. Be adventurous with your exercise program. Try a new sport today or find the three activities you enjoy the most and alternate between each of those over the course of a week. Keep exercising hard and maintain your discipline. But above all else, have a blast!

Part III: THE CHARACTER   *More Life Tips*

i)   Never discuss private or business matters inside elevators. You might be surprised who is standing next to you.

ii)   Set aside at least one night every week to be alone with your spouse. Turn off the TV and leave the answering machine on. Focus all your attention on your life partner. Really talk and enjoy the company of this very special person.

iii)   Experiment with new ideas. Try using an electronic scheduler or tool to see if it provides greater efficiency. Never stop improving. Stay hungry for new ideas.

iv)   Keep things in perspective-always. Things are never as bad as they might seem. Even the worst moments will pass. Challenges allow one to grow and become tougher.

v)   Do not make enemies.

vi)   Never take your family for granted. Think for a moment about how you would feel if your mother or father were no longer here. What thoughts have you forgotten to express, what loving gestures would you have performed? Now pick up the phone and tell these things to those you love.

Day 28

Date:_____

Part I: THE MIND   *Your Standards of Excellence*

In Day 20, you were exposed to the 5 Master Keys to making excellence your standard for life. Review them and make sure you are indeed applying them to every aspect of your life. Happiness does not come from relaxing and doing nothing. Happiness only comes from achieving and knowing that every day of your life you are getting better and better. Raise your standards and expect nothing but the very best from yourself. Life mastery is not for a chosen few. Slumbering deep inside you are powers and abilities that you cannot fathom. The leaders and achievers of the world all know this. Keep your aim high. Push yourself when you feel scared or lacking in motivation. Soon excellence will be your habit and aiming to the sky will be second nature to you.

Part II: THE BODY   *More Voice Conditioning*

On Day 5, a secret of longevity was shared with you: voice conditioning creates health. Practice the following exercises to further strengthen your voice:

      i)   Pronounce the following syllables as quickly and in as low a tone as possible: pe be me fe ve le re; ip ib iv if

      ii)   Sustain "humm" for as long as you can. Repeat 5 times.

      iii)   Say "haa" 5 times, each time exhaling deeply and releasing any tension that has built up inside your body.

Part III: THE CHARACTER   *Run Your Own Race*

One of the essential principles of life success and true personal mastery is to run your own race. Too often one gets caught up in what others are doing and what other people expect. "Why haven't you bought a house or started a family yet?" your lovely mother might ask. "You are too old to go to law school" your best friend might say. Set your goals, know what you want out of life and then plan methodically to take action on the path of your dreams. If you really know where you are going and cultivate the important habit of faith in yourself, what others say or think will mean very little to you. You are like a ship that has plotted its course. You know precisely the route on which you are travelling and the courses of other vessels are simply irrelevant. Running your own race also leads to peace of mind and self-confidence. If your school chum lands an early vice-presidency, you are genuinely thrilled for him because you are certain that you too will achieve your own goals in time. Pettiness vanishes and kindness towards others becomes one of your most notable personal traits.

Day 29

Date:_____

Part I: THE MIND   *Concentration Revisited*

This program has continually emphasized the importance of concentration in life mastery. Developing powerful concentration skills allows you to control the thoughts in your mind. Negative thoughts can then be banished and positive ones will then prevail. As a positive and motivated thinker, you will then have the desire and energy to achieve all that you are capable of achieving. If there is one secret you remember for the rest of your life, remember that true happiness and peace of mind can be developed. You can achieve the state of bliss by mastering the art of concentration.

Today, go back to Day 2 of the MegaLiving! program and practise the Burning Candle exercise for at least 25 minutes. You should have been practising your concentration exercises over the past few weeks and should be noticing dramatic improvements in this area. No longer will your mind wander at the slightest distraction. No longer will you become annoyed at the most trivial of events. You no longer major in minor things and now focus only on the very best in life.

Part II: THE BODY   *Food For Thought*

It is now beyond debate that what you put into your body affects your mind. Eat too much meat and other hard to digest foods and you will feel lazy and feel less alert. Eat light foods such as vegetables and fresh fruits and you will soon have boundless energy and will be startlingly attentive and mentally agile. Moods are even affected by some foods. The essential point is to strictly monitor what goes in so your mind is given the very best fuel it deserves.

Make a list of all the food you have ingested over the past 24 hours. Now remove as much of the fatty foods as possible. Try replacing chocolate bars and snack foods with fresh fruit or yogurt. Cut down your red meat intake as much as you can as this food is exceptionally hard to digest which takes up an undue amount of your energy. Once you precisely identify what you are eating, you can take steps to improve the quality of your food and then the quality of your physical life.

Part III: THE CHARACTER   *The Importance of the Mastermind*

The Mastermind is a term that has been used in business circles to describe a group of people assembled to motivate one another, to brainstorm for new ideas and to support each other as each participant tries new ventures. You have clearly committed yourself to self-mastery and achieving all you can. By getting to Day 29 of the 30 day MegaLiving! program you have demonstrated your discipline and enthusiasm for success in life. Today, plan your own Personal Mastery Mastermind. Think of the four most positive people you know, people who live with zest and are determined to enjoy their dreams, people who are open to new ideas and who you can trust. Discuss the Mastermind concept with them and plan to meet at least once every two weeks. At these meetings, brainstorm for ideas on personal excellence techniques, ways to live with more passion, tools for time management and financial success. Motivate one another and use the powers of synergy to catapult you to results you have never seen before. The Personal Mastery Mastermind is one of the most effective resources you will ever have to start and continue MegaLiving!

Day 30

Date:_____

The Conclusion of MegaLiving!, the Ultimate Action-Plan for Mastery of Your Mind, Body and Character

Congratulations to you for successfully completing the 30 day program. You have been exposed to some of the very best of the world's secrets for personal excellence and life mastery. Others have applied these strategies and have gone on to find enormous personal wealth, true peace of mind and perfect health. Success in life is now yours for the taking!

This, the final day of the MegaLiving! program, is not the end but really the start of a new way of life for you. Over the past 30 days, you have learned exceptionally powerful principles and exercises to control the way you think and feel. You should be feeling more motivated, energized and disciplined than you have felt in the past. In this book are all the secrets for lasting success and happiness. Practise the concepts and share them with others. Do not stop using the program but, rather, make it an essential part of your life. An elite athlete does not stop conditioning after the first race is over but maintains a training regimen over many years until it is second nature. MegaLiving! should be a way of life for you too. Every day you will improve in some way and find a new sparkle of happiness and fun. Happiness is truly not a goal but a way of travelling through this incredibly wonderful world.

You have devoted much time to excelling with this program and have made sacrifices along the way. You are now equipped to achieve any dream you have ever had. Believe in yourself and your potential. Shatter any limitations and appreciate that any challenge can indeed be overcome. Dream higher than you have ever dreamt before and aim for the stars. I wish you well and hope that we can one day meet on this path of success that we share. This path is open for everyone, supremely exciting and filled with magnificent gifts. This path is called MegaLiving!

Robin S. Sharma
April 1, 1994

MegaLiving! SuccessLog

© Robin S. Sharma, 1994

Every day, in every way, I am getting Better and Better.

Emile Coue

| | The Mind | The Body | The Character |

Days of The Program	A	B	C
1			
2			
3			
4			
5			
6			
7			
8			
9			
10			
11			
12			
13			
14			
15			
16			
17			
18			
19			
20			
21			
22			
23			
24			
25			
26			
27			
28			
29			
30			

MegaLiving! Notes & Progress

ABOUT THE AUTHOR

Robin Sharma, LL.B., LL.M., is a 29 year old litigation lawyer, author, professional speaker and personal excellence consultant. He practises law in the Civil Litigation Section of the Canadian Justice Department. *MegaLiving! 30 Days to a Perfect Life* is his first book.

Mr. Sharma received his Bachelor of Law (LL.B.) degree from Dalhousie University in Halifax, Nova Scotia. In 1989, he made Canadian legal history in being selected as the first Judicial Law Clerk to the Nova Scotia Court of Appeal. Mr. Sharma went on to be named as a Foundation Scholar by the Law Foundation of Nova Scotia and was awarded a full graduate scholarship to pursue advanced legal studies. In 1990, Robin Sharma received a Master of Laws degree (LL.M.) from Canada's oldest law school, Dalhousie Law School. He later moved to the nation's capital to serve the federal Justice Department as a constitutional lawyer specializing in the *Charter of Rights & Freedoms*.

Mr. Sharma has published numerous scholarly articles on varied topics ranging from the Canadian Constitution to the benefits of alternative means of dispute resolution in resolving litigation before the courts. His work has appeared in the prestigious *National Journal of Constitutional Law* and in the *Nova Scotia Law Times*, amongst other publications. Mr. Sharma has also been a featured speaker at legal seminars including those of the Canadian Bar Association and conferences sponsored by the Justice Department. He is a member of both the Nova Scotia and Ontario Bars.

Robin Sharma is a practitioner of the ancient martial art of Tae Kwon Do, has skydived, played in a popular university rock and roll band and has successfully completed his first triathlon. Mr. Sharma is currently working on his second book, *The Youthful Lawyer - 10 Ancient Master Secrets of the Fountain of Youth* and lives in Toronto, Canada with his wife and son.

Speaking Engagements & Corporate Seminars

Robin Sharma is a dynamic and entertaining public speaker. For more information, please write to:

> **The Haunsla Corporation**
> **Suite 957, 7B Pleasant Boulevard,**
> **Toronto, Ontario**
> **Canada**
> **M4T 1K2**

MegaLiving! 30 Days to a Perfect Life

Order Form

Further copies of *MegaLiving! 30 Days to a Perfect Life* are available in better bookstores or if you prefer, you may send a copy of this order form to us and receive *MegaLiving!* by 1st Class Mail.

Forward your rush order with Cheque/money order payable in the name of The Haunsla Corporation to:

> MegaLiving! Special Book Offer
> Suite 957,
> 7B Pleasant Blvd.,
> Toronto, Ontario
> Canada
> M4T 1K2

NAME & ADDRESS IN BLOCK LETTERS PLEASE

Name _____

Address _____

_____

_____

Number of Copies Required: _____

Total Cost @ only $19.97 each: _____

Postage, service & handling: <u>Included</u>

The author will make every possible effort to sign your copy of this powerful book. Kindly allow 2-6 weeks for delivery.

Quantities Are Limited

It is our sincere hope that you have received tremendous benefits from this revolutionary personal mastery program. We also offer the following to further assist you in MegaLiving! & reaching your Perfect Life:

The MegaLiving! Seminar: Achieving Life Mastery

This incredible seminar incorporates all of the elements of the MegaLiving! 30 day program and provides you will all of the dynamic tools and strategies to take your life to the highest level & make it a wonderful masterpiece. It is offered throughout Canada & The United States (special corporate seminars available). Asian dates also available schedule permitting.

MegaLiving! 30 Days to a Perfect Life: The Audio Program
($39.95 CDN)

At last, one of the very best personal mastery programs is available to you on tape by 1st Class mail. Live the secrets and strategies of the MegaLiving! 30 day program for a perfect life as the author enthusiastically takes you through the dynamic essentials of the plan and concepts. You also learn the guiding principles of MegaLiving!, the 5 secrets of longevity and youthfulness and the 200 MasterSecrets of Success. Do not miss this time limited offer. Order today!

MegaPower! The Monthly Self-Mastery Report ($99.95 CDN)

This powerful monthly report will keep you up to date with the very latest information and ideas to keep you motivated and on the path to a perfect life of self-mastery. MegaPower! has sections on the achievement of excellence in all 3 of the key areas of your life: your Mind, Body & Character. This report is like no other & ensures that you keep MegaLiving! (10 incredible issues per year)

For more information on these products, please write to:

MegaLiving! 30 Days to a Perfect Life
Suite 957
7B Pleasant Blvd.,
Toronto, Ontario
Canada
M4T 1K2